Daniel Häni

Philip Kovce

Voting for Freedom

Albert Wenger (Foreword)

Joseph F. Bailey (Translation)

Daniel Häni is Entrepreneur. He is Co-Founder and CEO of Switzerland's biggest Coffee-House "unternehmen mitte," as well as Co-Initiator of the Swiss popular initiative for an unconditional basic income. The initiative was successfully submitted in 2013, and received media responses worldwide.

Philip Kovce is Associated Research Fellow at the Chair of Economics and Philosophy at Witten/Herdecke University, Germany's first private university. He is a member of "tt30," the Club of Rome's young leaders Think Tank, and works for several German newspapers as well as broadcasters.

Albert Wenger is a Managing Partner at Union Square Ventures in New York City. Union Square Ventures invests in Internet businesses, including companies such as Twitter, Etsy, Twilio, and Soundcloud. Albert studied Economics and Computer Science at Harvard University and holds a PhD in Information Technology from the Massachusetts Institute of Technology.

Joseph F. Bailey teaches German literature, as well as English as a second language to high-school students in Germany. He also works as a freelance translator, and is currently translating the works of Robert Sardello. Joseph holds a PhD in German literature from the University of Michigan.

Those who expect to reap the blessings of freedom, must, like men, undergo the fatigues of supporting it.

Thomas Paine

Published by First World Development
Gerbergasse 30, CH-4001 Basel
www.first-world-development.org
© 2016 Daniel Häni, Philip Kovce
All rights reserved.

This book was first published in German:
Daniel Häni, Philip Kovce:
Was fehlt, wenn alles da ist?
Warum das bedingungslose Grundeinkommen
die richtigen Fragen stellt
© 2015 Orell Füssli Verlag AG, Zurich
All rights reserved by and controlled
through Orell Füssli Verlag AG.
www.ofv.ch

Editor: Troy Vine, Berlin
Cover: Tobias Handorf, Basel
Layout: Nigel Grünwaldt, Göttingen
Print: CreateSpace Independent Publishing,
North Charleston

1ˢᵗ Edition 2016

Printed in the United States of America

ISBN 978-1523711277

Daniel Häni
Philip Kovce

Foreword by Albert Wenger
Translated from German into English by Joseph F. Bailey

VOTING FOR FREEDOM

The 2016 Swiss Referendum on Basic Income:
A Milestone in the Advancement of Democracy

▶▶ **fwd** First World Development

Table of Contents

Intermezzo I

All Those Opposed   61

2 Power

Who's the Boss when Everyone is the Boss?   73

Why the Popular Initiative is the Right Path 74 | Beyond Party Politics 75 | The Citizen as Sovereign 76 | Not More, just Better Regulation 78 | Switzerland, Germany, the USA 79 | Basic Income for Politicians 82 | One for All, All for One 84 | The Conditions of the Unconditional 86 | We Are (Not) Family 87 | Emancipation for Everyone 89 | Working Capacity as Welfare Benefit 91 | What Is Fair? 93 | Who little Risks becomes Reckless 94 | Who will Come when Basic Income Comes? 96 | Basic Income as Property 98 | And Who is Going to Pay for it All? 100 | The Redistribution of Power 103

Intermezzo II

All Those In Favor   105

3 Freedom

How Free Are We if We Stop Coercing Others?   117

Epilog

What's Next   153

Appendix

Foreword by Albert Wenger

As a venture investor I have a front row seat to innovation and thus to the ongoing transformation of the economy and society. From that perch it could not be any clearer: We are headed for a major transition. One that is as profound as when we went from the forager age to the agrarian age and then from the agrarian age to the industrial age. Each time, how society is organized shifted profoundly.

At the heart of this new transition is digital technology. Digital is fundamentally different from what came before in two ways: universality and zero marginal cost. A computer is a universal machine that can compute anything that is computable in our universe. We know this thanks to the groundbreaking work of Alan Turing. And we now see it at work. We have had a series of breakthroughs in machine learning that have given us computer programs that can recognize faces better than humans, drive cars, diagnose disease.

Because of the zero marginal cost of digital technology we can make these capabilities available to anyone anywhere in the world for free. We already know this to be true for digital content such as Wikipedia and Youtube. But it also applies to a digital diagnosis system. This means that we are on the brink of making the initial healthcare step—figuring out what is wrong—affordable and accessible to all of humanity.

This kind of automation has historically been a good thing. If we did not automate many of the tasks in agriculture, we would all still be working in the fields. Now though, many people see automation as a threat. We have constructed so much of our individual lives and our collective culture and economy around work. The prospect that we might be able to automate much of it scares people instead of liberating them.

In this important book, Daniel Häni and Philip Kovce explore the many questions that we have to answer so that we can become comfortable and embrace the future that is now possible. They discuss a proposal known as basic income, which separates work from the need to earn a living by paying everyone a guaranteed amount. With basic income people can choose freely how to spend their time. Basic income turns more automation from a threat to people's livelihood to a promise of a freer future.

Switzerland will be holding a referendum on June 5th, 2016 to add basic income to the Swiss constitution. This vote represents a historic opportunity for social and economic progress. By embracing basic income in a peaceful vote, Switzerland could lead the way for others to follow. Daniel and Philip make a compelling case for why Swiss citizens should vote to support basic income. Readers all around the world can find why they too should support basic income in their own countries in addition to the Swiss initiative.

What's at Stake

Questions change everything. What would you do if your income were taken care of? Once a person has taken this question to heart, nothing is the same as before. Life runs a different course. There's no going back to the way things were before.

Whoever asks questions is placing something in question. What was considered self-evident is now no longer valid. At least its no longer self-evident. Questions put old things off balance and impart gravity to new things. They provide an opportunity to speak one's mind and to come to agreements. They pave the way into the future that we want to travel together.

Good questions are the best answers, as they do not force an answer on anyone. Good questions condense and expand. They put straight what is at stake and leave open what the next step is supposed to be. We interact with each other all the better, the better the questions are that we delve into.

*   *   *

The Swiss popular initiative for an unconditional basic income poses questions. In doing so, however, it is not asking about details, but about basics. It's not about setting a minimum wage or placing limits on maximum income; it's neither about the sales tax on a steak sold in a canteen as opposed to one sold in a high class restaurant, nor about radio and television broadcasting fees, nor speed limits or tax privileges; rather, it's about deciding which direction to take.

The Swiss popular initiative asks two things. Firstly: What do I actually want? What would I do if I didn't have to worry about earning an income for myself? What do I devote my time and energy to when I'm granted the freedom to decide for myself? That's the question that throws me back on myself. It addresses me as a self-determined individual. What is at stake is the image I have of myself.

The second question is: Am I willing to grant others unconditionally the fundamental things they need to live on? Can I imagine their receiving a basic income without first having to meet stipulations or perform services of any kind? Am I willing to let others make decisions concerning their own lives? This question is about other people as self-determined individuals. What is at stake is the image I have of them.

If unconditional basic income were adopted by a monarch, a government or a parliament, its impact would be much smaller than the impact of an entire elective population grappling with the questions basic income asks. We cannot delegate these questions, as they are about us. That's why it makes sense for us to put it to popular vote.

*   *   *

What's missing when it's all here? This question asserts itself in the face of lack in abundance, of poverty in wealth, of emptiness in plenitude. We pursue this question in three chapters, which deal with the way we comprehend work, power and freedom: What would you do if everyone else worked for you? Who's the boss when everyone is the boss? How free are we if we stop coercing others?

This book began as play: Every evening over the course of several weeks, we asked each other a question about basic income. The following day we gave each other an answer. These answers laid the cornerstone for this book. It is a book of statements in constant search of pointed emphasis; a book of paragraphs that condenses thought from passage to passage; and it is a book of essays containing chapter-by-chapter enlightenment of the phenomena it deals with.

Authors who know it all either shame their readers or bore them. The remedies for know-it-alls are humor and skepticism. And so we have done no more than formulate questions with a twinkle in the eye; questions that do not make basic income seem like a patent solution, to be sure; but which show it as a kind of master key to provide access to the questions that move the present day. Ideologies come our way as answers. Basic income, as long as it is not an ideology, comes our way with its questions.

What Would You Do if Everyone Else Worked for You?

The Reality of the Division of Labor

We work. We have never not worked. But the way we organize our work, the status it has, the idea we form of it—all that is in a constant state of change. Before, our counterpart was nature. It challenged us as it fed us. We developed at its hands and along with it. Today, our main counterpart is technology. Technology challenges us as well, while it also serves us. In the future, we will more and more stand opposite ourselves and the selves of the other people. After all, we stand opposite everything that we cannot control or calculate. The fact that it will come to this is one of the success stories of the division of labor.

What does division of labor mean? Division of labor means that no one any longer does everything by themselves. Division of labor means that we divide the processes of production and of providing services into individual steps. This enables the development of know-how and increases work productivity. Division of labor is what has led us from self-supply to external supply.

As self-sufficient, I worked for myself. Under the conditions of external supply, I work for others. With self-sufficiency, the fruits of my labor were for me, my family, my clan. What I brought home from the hunt I ate myself. What I harvested from the field was for my own livelihood. I consumed what I had first produced.

Today, in times of worldwide external supply through division of labor, things are different: I work for others and no longer for myself; and others work for me and no longer for themselves. My work now has only a small part in the product. I may be in the human resources department of a large company and responsible for hiring new employees. Or I am a teacher; I train young people and prepare them for what they will do in times to come. Maybe I'm a truck driver and assist in the distribution of many different products by transporting them every day. In all these cases I no longer directly consume what I produce. This is the largest work-related turn of events in human history.

We might give the division of labor as it has come to be in our times the name "structural charity." It no longer takes moral prompting to be social or charitable and to allow others to take part in our own success. No. Things are simply set up in such a way that we always work for others. It doesn't get more social than that. Be that as it may, we still think that because we get paid for our work we work for ourselves. We think the wages we receive for doing work for others is the prey we bring home from the hunt. We confuse wages with the purpose of our work. While in former times we hunted, today we enter the job market, grab the first acceptable job we can get and treat the money we get for it like quarry—like a bear we bagged in the thicket.

What is it, then, that we need to understand? We need to understand that nowadays I live from the work others do for me. The other people are no longer my enemies and my rivals; rather, they are my friends and manufacturers. Enemies compete, friends cooperate. If nobody worked for me, I wouldn't have anything. I would revert to self-sufficiency. That is yesterday's present.

What follows from this? If I live from work that others perform for me, it is worth my while to make sure they are glad to work for me. If I want to consume good products, I have to make sure they can be produced under good working conditions. I have to see to it that the people who work for me can do so in the best possible way.

"Selfishness is not a different world—just a smaller one," says Swiss author Ludwig Hohl. According to Hohl, selfishness "is not the opposite of flourishing within the world, but rather a preliminary to it."[1] It's no use decrying the selfishness of our times. We don't need to demonize it; we need to understand it. Then it transforms, even mentally, into what it has been for quite some time already: structural charity.

Complete Emptiness

We live today in abundance. From the hunters and gatherers to the high cultures of Antique times and on into the Middle Ages, the Renaissance, the Enlightenment, the Industrial Revolution, even into the first half of the 20th century—the law of lack held sway. A few powerful people did well, but not even they had hot running water, private jets or smartphones.

From Aristotle's teachings on household management to the modern precursors of political economics such as Adam Smith, David Ricardo or Léon Walras—the presupposition of their economic theories has always been lack. Today many people still do suffer under not being provided the means to meet their basic needs. However, lack has long since ceased being a necessity. It has become, as has abundance, our own creation.[2]

If we have the capacity to feed more people than currently inhabit the earth and innumerable people still suffer hunger, it is because we treat wealth as if it were rare, a scarce good, a limited resource. What we are missing is the ability to deal in an appropriate manner with the abundance that actually exists.

The discipline demanded of us by abundance is generosity. Those incapable of it become voracious or greedy—two modes of behavior in the face of lack. Basic income takes seriously the fact that lack has ceased to exist and frees us from having to feel it subjectively in the wrong place. Whoever sees themselves permanently threatened by material dearth races throughout the world like an animal in search of food. They either snatch their prey away from their own kind, or eat willingly out of their master's hand.

Basic income exposes the animalistic attitude of self-sufficiency. Only humans are capable of comprehensive external supply. Of course division of labor exists among animals too. But only human beings are able to place the satisfaction of their basic needs fully into the hands of fellow human beings. A state of affairs made an everyday occurrence by the Industrial Revolution.

French sociologist Georges Bataille was one of the first to formulate a theory of abundance. According to Bataille, abundance expresses itself in one of two ways: Either it is wasteful, as is the case with art, or it is destructive, as with terror attacks.[3]

Basic income makes it possible for abundance to find expression not just in wastefulness and destruction, but also in fruitfulness. For lack and abundance are ultimately two forms of being at a loss: Lack doesn't know where to get things, while abundance doesn't know what to do with the things it has.

German philosopher Peter Sloterdijk depicts unconditional basic income as an approach, "which helps modern society to leave behind the Ancient Regime of lack and artificially created scarcity."[4] If we can succeed at that, we will have voluntarily become generous.

People with No Money Harm the Economy

For people who live in abundance, the problem is not producing, but selling what they produce. The shelves are full. Everything is there. To ensure that it also gets sold, advertising has become a huge sector of the economy. For everything, in every place and using all means, a market needs to be found. How do we get more customers? How do we win their loyalty? How can we sell them even more products? There is no talk of production problems.

A recession occurs not when we produce less, but when our purchasing power diminishes. Even for the new iPhone demand exceeds supply for only a few hours or days. And even that is nothing but an advertising ploy in which a shortage is orchestrated. No one says on account of too great a demand that we have an unsolvable problem. We are far more afraid of demand decreasing than not being able to meet it.

Producing more of something is no problem. Producing less is likelier to be one. The hardest thing for a business is to shrink. As long as demand is greater than production, it is usually possible to adjust quickly and at no great risk. One's business is growing, after all. But if the demand decreases it truly is an entrepreneurial challenge to pull back on production without having to book a loss.

We behave as if we were living in lack. But there is far too much of far too many things! Economic crisis is when we have too little money to be able to consume. The problem is not unemployment, but lack of income. The downward spiral of a financial crisis begins with a lack of sales. If sales are too low, many people lose their jobs, and the result is that more people consume even less, for which reason even more people lose their jobs. They are doomed to the ranks of the unemployed.

In such a situation unconditional basic income is an effective program for fiscal stimulus. It would immediately spur the faltering economies of Spain, Greece, Portugal, Italy or France. The moment people have enough money with which to consume, they stimulate production. The consumer is the economy's employer; if the consumer falters, so does the economy. Anyone unable to buy is economically worthless. People with no money harm the economy. The economy would break down if a political movement were to form that successfully demanded that nothing be purchased any longer.

At present, China is introducing more social benefits in order to reduce its savings rates. This way, it is hoped that Chinese citizens will stop hoarding the country's capital and bring more of it into circulation.[5] Switzerland has the highest savings rate for private households in all of Europe—with Germany hot on its heels.[6] Unconditional basic income could make savings rates drop, since it guarantees the very same minimum financial security for the sake of which people hold on to money rather than spend it.

What drives production is demand, which leads to buying. What we need to guarantee is not production, but income. No income, no economy. Unconditional basic income secures overall income, and in the process causes a long-term stabilization of the economy.

Creating Jobs is not Social, but Antisocial

There is as much work as there are people. Work is not something that can be distributed fairly. What is unfair, though, is hindering people from working. But just that is what happens when we treat work as if it were a commodity to be bought and sold and thus use it as a means of barter. Work itself is not a commodity; rather, it is what first creates commodities. The great tragedy of the establishment of gainful employment is that it links work with income. Basic income dissolves this connection between work and financial security and brings our rigidified notion of work back into a state of flow.

Why shouldn't work be distributed fairly? Why should working time be shortened? Is it because work is a scarce commodity? Does it need to be distributed better? If people depend on work for their livelihood, the answer is yes. We call those people unemployed who look for work because they need an income in order to survive. They ask for work. And if they are lucky, some "generous" person gives them a job. This is what things have come to. And then we say, "thank you for letting me work for you." Or in the store, "thank you for buying from us." We say thank you to someone who gives something to us or does something for us, yet we don't say: "Thank you for letting me bake you the cake that you now get to take home."

When we buy a cake, we ought to say: "Thanks for the cake! Thank you for baking it for me, and many thanks to all the people who helped you so that you could bake it for me. Thanks to the person who supplied the flour, to the miller, the farmer—thanks to the whole world."

We live in an upside-down world in which those who take something demand gratitude and those who give something say thank you. The reason: We have turned work into a limited commodity. The very concept of work is upside-down. Its head lies on the ground; its feet hang up in the air. The result: We suffer under our abundance. We tread on our thoughts with our feet. We produce without using our heads, without taking into account what we truly need.

A lot of people who simply leave their trash lying in public places, when asked why they don't dispose of it properly, say they sense themselves not as perpetrators of a misdemeanor, but rather as benefactors. After all, by littering they are creating jobs. And these offenders are right. Except that creating jobs is not social, but antisocial! It ensures that other people have to deal with our garbage. Not creating work is social, but doing away with it. Not the people who leave their trash lying around for others to take care of are social, but rather the people who dispose of it and in so doing spare others this task. And that applies not just to garbage.

Fulltime Employment or Meaningful Activity?

By continuing current politics of push and pull, full employment is achievable according to job market authorities. Job market authorities would do anything to cut the unemployment rate. But what lies behind the ideal of full employment?

By conventional definition, full employment is a state in which all people in a given country who are willing to engage in gainful employment are indeed gainfully employed. Whoever is looking for a job but is unable to find one is considered to be unemployed. A few of the many factors that figure into the chances that a person has on the job market are age, qualifications and residency. The goal is to be employed rather than unemployed. "For us, full employment is no mere unattainable utopia; it is a political objective," says Rolf Zimmermann, former general secretary of the Swiss Federation of Trade Unions.[7] And it is German chancellor Angela Merkel's opinion that "employment for everyone is an objective we should all keep in mind."[8]

In 1995, a conference took place in San Francisco at the behest of the Gorbachev Foundation, to which a group of leading politicians, entrepreneurs and scientists were invited for the purpose of thinking about the future. The main topic of this conference was the proposition that in the 21st century a mere twenty per cent of the population would be enough to keep the world economy in motion.

American economist Jeremy Rifkin is considered a mastermind of the so-called 20/80 society. In his bestseller *The End of Work*, he analyzes the consequences of technological progress and comes to the conclusion that work will do away with itself. According to Rifkin, millions and millions of jobs will be eliminated both by progressing rationalization and by the world-wide implementation of information technology. He states that: "Artificial intelligence and speech recognition programs are replacing increasing amounts of office jobs. Merchandising has become a different field; here, the trend is more and more away from physical and toward digital sales. Even attorneys, accountants or radiologists have become anxious [...] We will lose our jobs to machines and algorithms; it's happening as we speak!"[9] Dirk Helbing, a physicist at the Swiss Federal Institute of Technology in Zurich, emphasizes the dynamics of this process: "Nothing will stay the same as it was! In most of the countries in Europe about 50% of today's jobs will be lost."[10]

Rifkin claims the logic has been refuted which states that technological progress and increased productivity will render old jobs obsolete, but will also create at least as many new jobs as it eliminates. For him the question is not whether or not the 20/80 society is coming, but much rather how we are to adjust to it when it comes: "Redefining the role of the individual in a society absent of mass formal work is, perhaps, the seminal issue of the coming age," thus Rifkin in 1995.[11]

There are a lot of people who do not share Rifkin's prognosis. They tend more to agree with Robert Solow, the Nobel Prize laureate for economics, who believes that, "fear of the automation of the work world is just as unfounded as the fear of colliding with a gigantic asteroid."[12] Rifkin's critics argue as follows: Since the human life-span is becoming longer and we are reproducing less, there will be an unprecedented shortage of skilled labor. They say that fewer and fewer employed people will have to care and produce for more and more unemployable people, which would lead not to job losses, but rather to an unexpected demand for jobs.

Regardless of what work humans and machines will perform, the goal of full employment is misguided. This is because full employment degrades work to mere employment. We only work when there is something to do. Employment is something we seek even when there is nothing to get done.

The notion of full employment stems from the fact that we secure our existence by means of income-producing activity. People who work receive an income. That is why the claim that we need gainful employment is more important than the question of the way we work and of what we want to do. No matter how, no matter what: What matters is that one is employed. Gainful employment in connection with insurance and pension benefits is what nowadays we call the absolute best.

Full employment epitomizes the misguided notion that work exists for the purpose of employing people. Work is not something we create or secure; it's something we do. People who are meaningfully active become active when something needs to be done. And there is always something to be done, though not in the form of paid employment, which is decreasing at a growing rate. This is why Theo Wehner, an industrial psychologist at Zurich's Swiss Federal Institute of Technology, concludes that "the idea of full employment is more utopian than that of basic income."[13]

What's Missing when Skilled Labor is Lacking?

People are getting older; machines are getting better. Where that is taking us isn't clear yet. Jeremy Rifkin and others are speaking of the end of work. Rationalization and digitalization liberate us from tedious activity, or so the theory goes. On the other hand, we are experiencing a growing shortage of skilled labor. Even today we are short on engineers, computer scientists, doctors, nurses, teachers. And as time passes we'll be even shorter. What does this mean?

Unconditional basic income finances a training for everyone to become specialists of living their own life, a lifelong learning process. This is no end in itself. The only people capable of being truly active for others are those who are fully independent. People who specialize in themselves are better able to recognize what the others need. This is the particular boom in skilled labor that could be set off by basic income.

But what about the skilled workers who even today businesses say are lacking? What about the jobs nobody does? There are different reasons for a lack in offer despite existing demand for it. In all cases, the reason has to do with the lack of attractiveness of the task to be done. Either it pays too poorly or people prefer different tasks for other reasons. Another possible reason is that such activities are no longer organized via the labor market, but rather privately—between neighbors and friends.

The objectivity of the shortage in skilled labor is oftentimes a subjective one. Businesses that pay less than workers ask suffer skilled labor shortages. Whereas employers who pay well needn't worry. The same holds for respect and acknowledgement: Someone who sees that their activity is esteemed and appreciated, and who furthermore enjoys meeting with colleagues will continue practicing their occupation.

Unconditional basic income makes it possible to do or refrain from doing anything, or to do anything in a completely different way. It enables us to care for our aging or ailing loved ones outside the nursing home, to get an education beyond the university, to install software for our friends or a gas range for our neighbors. Anyone unwilling to indulge this privatization will have to support jobs that are important to them in a way that others will still want to do them on a commercial basis. Corporations will no longer invest in glossy brochures and marketing, but in a social work atmosphere, in family-friendly part time positions, in time off for vacation during school holidays, and in an adequate salary.

Or they will invest in automatization that renders a lot of activities obsolete—including in the service sector. In technological terms, there is less and less that stands in the way of this. If we consider replacing humans with machines an ethical problem, we will either have to arouse other peoples' passion for remaining active despite the technological possibilities to rationalize jobs, or we will have to do without services we cannot perform ourselves.

Unconditional basic income reacts to the elimination of great numbers of jobs by not guaranteeing a job, but guaranteeing income. This comes close to the practice of the welfare state as it is known chiefly in the Scandinavian countries, where not companies, but rather workers are saved from bankruptcy. While Germany props up Opel and so doing interferes massively with the market, Sweden doesn't bail out Saab, but its workers instead. They call that "flexicurity": flexibility and security.[14]

Unconditional basic income makes it possible to engage in risky activities, since it removes the risk of existing. It makes it possible to help where help is needed. And thanks to basic income, shortages worth receiving aid can be distinguished from shortages that are no more than distortions of the job market.

What Follows Automatically?

The automation of the world is both a blessing and a curse. The blessing is easy to discern: Robots, machines, computer programs, in short the whole process of automation takes the hard, often boring and monotonous work off our hands. And that's not all. Soon it will be possible for our cars to operate without drivers, to replace doctors with diagnostic applications, to replace caregivers with robots, which never become impatient or angry, and are also in service round the clock. The Care-O-bot, being developed by the Fraunhofer Institute for Manufacturing Engineering and Automation, is admittedly still in the prototype stage of its development, but it is no longer a question of whether such an invention is possible; but when.[15] To be sure, robotic seals are controversial, but they are already being put to use successfully in Japan. They're cuddly, they respond to touch and are quite popular among dementia patients. A blessing or a curse?[16]

For those still unable to visualize what we're in for, the Swedish television series *Real Humans* points in the general direction. *Real Humans* anticipates issues we will be faced with in the near future. In this television series, robots appear that are called hubots (human robots). They permeate our everyday life, the business world and our leisure activities. It is even possible to issue a copy of a human that can be uploaded to a hubot. Hubots require neither food nor drink nor sleep nor a basic income. All they need is electricity. And they can be switched off.

At all events, the blessing of automation is that our services are no longer needed as cogs in the machinery of industrialization, and that we are placed before the question of how we wish to be active in a meaningful way. Acting as if we were still necessary for manning assembly lines is not the right response. It would be tragic if we were to ignore this grand success story and continue to force hard work and sweat on ourselves. The question reads as follows: How can we place technological progress at our service?

From this point of view, we can understand unconditional basic income as an automation dividend. Robots don't need unconditional basic income; we do. We receive the wages for the work robots do instead of us, because they don't need wages. We reward ourselves for having invented robots. Basic income shares with every citizen the earnings generated by technological progress. It does this by granting to each individual subjective access to the freedom that technological progress has long since objectively realized.

Work-Life Schizophrenia

When we live, we do so unceasingly. Whether as children in day-care or as seniors in a nursing home; whether as a mother at home or as a father in an executive chair; whether while sunbathing or on the career ladder: We are alive, and as living beings we feel sometimes better, sometimes worse. The time we live is our life-time.

Drawing a distinction between working time and free time is a relatively recent phenomenon. It was unknown to the citizens of ancient Athens. They always had free time—their slaves always had working time. That was their lives. On a medieval farm, it was working time as long as there was something to do, and free time when the work was finished. Maximizing working time or pretending to work were not what mattered; what mattered was getting the job done. It was not until the advent of the division of labor and so-called alienated work, which in the wake of industrialization attracted hordes of workers to the factories, that a separation was made between working time and free time. Today the name given to this phenomenon is work-life balance.

Anyone wishing to maintain a balance between work and life clings to the outdated division that stems from the industrial age. They separate work from life and themselves from work. They resolve not to work too much and not to live too little. The concern for good work and a good life leads to job stress and to family stress.

The separation between work and life has become a widespread disease: work-life schizophrenia. Whoever does not think of working time as life time belongs to the past: Every single hour we spend with ourselves and with others is, after all, an entry in the book of a person's life. Whoever doesn't notice that becomes ill.

We devalue work if we do not see it as life time. Even worse: We devalue ourselves along with what we do on the job. Whoever engages in a job now in order to have a nice life later on has no life. Whoever submits to a job in order to attain freedom remains unfree.

Just as we do not perceive working time as life time, in the same way we are unable to appreciate the everyday tasks we perform in our free time in the family or in the neighborhood, without asking for money or even being asked to do them. Mothers who drive their children to school, fathers who help with homework, the person who provides care for a sick friend, unsalaried people who do meaningful work on a voluntary basis—they all do these things not for money, but out of love for their fellow human beings.

When we take hold of things that need to be done, when we take an initiative that is called for, we live and work. Work-life balance turns work into something smaller than it is—namely, into mere duty at the front; it turns life into something smaller than it is— namely, into mere free time; and it makes us into something smaller than we are—namely, into half-entities who some of the time are busy and some of the time are lazy.

Working time and free time are life time. To distinguish between them is to make work unfree and free time unproductive. Today it would be possible both to live in freedom and to work. Whoever hinders that squanders the capital of the future: the free human being.

In a Hell of a Mess or: If You Don't Eat, You Can't Work

"If anyone would not work, neither should he eat."[17] These are familiar words of St. Paul in the New Testament. What, precisely, they meant in the Apostle's times is a story of its own.[18] They have at any rate survived to this day and long since become a moralistic threat: Nothing comes from nothing. Since there are many things we need and since we can only provide what we collectively produce, shirkers deserve to be punished.

Whoever thinks in this manner thinks poorly. For millennia we have told our own story as a story of dearth, of shortage, of lack. More precisely: as a story of gains in knowledge and of losses of food. Adam and Eve eat from the Tree of Knowledge and gain knowledge but remain hungry. As their punishment, they are forced to leave Paradise. According to God's sentence, Adam has to earn his bread by the sweat of his brow and Eve has to bear children in great pain. This is the archetypal biblical scene of pain, lack and knowledge.

There is also an entirely different creation story to be told: At this story's beginning stands not punishment, but rather a gift. For one God or another, the creation is proof of their strength, beneficence, perfection or imperfection, of their might, their freedom, their aloneness or their love. In each case, the first human being receives the world as a gift. And how are human beings to treat this gift?

Gifts leave us free. We cannot be forced either to receive them or to reciprocate. We behave today as if every single person coming into the world were first supposed to earn their existence, and not as if they were welcome simply because they were born. The fact that expectations of this kind exist bears witness to an age in which work is deemed necessary, but often also superfluous and senseless at the same time. Only those who do not love doing an activity and who do not see that carrying it out is necessary refuse to engage in it. Nowadays it is often nearly impossible to see that one is needed, because we already have everything; it's all been here for quite some time. And yet we act as if everyone first has to prove how hardworking they are if they are to receive a piece of the oversized cake.

The saying that we can only distribute what we have produced is as trivial as the present-day conclusion drawn from it is fatal. The conclusion is: Everybody has to act as if they were producing something in order to take part, instead of simply being allowed to take part. Only those allowed to take part know what really needs to be done. Those not allowed to take part act as if they could see what needs to be done, so that they might be permitted to take part. This is the slanted view that is unable to look at the tasks at hand but is nevertheless forced to keep an eye on income. Basic income helps people to see tasks at hand more clearly, because it alleviates them of having to keep their gaze fixed on the income produced.

Paradise on Earth or: Anyone Unwilling to Think is Fired

"First comes food, then morality."[19] Or so it says in Bertolt Brecht's *Threepenny Opera*. He got that notion by observing how life is determined by dearth, as well as how people are often expected to do noble deeds instead of first quelling their hunger. Only when someone has had enough to eat can they be productive. Denying food to those who refuse to make themselves useful is the way of the Old Testament: an eye for an eye, a tooth for a tooth. In the New Testament it says: If someone strikes you on your right cheek, turn the other cheek to that person. This means that punishers also punish themselves by robbing the punished of the opportunity to become better. No one made to do things they do not like in order to survive becomes a better person. No confession becomes truer if it is coerced by means of torture.

A return to Paradise is by no means excluded in the Biblical narrative. How does this return to Paradise work? It works by grasping conceptually the paradisiacal circumstances that we have long since created materially. Here and today. Nature and technology give us light, warmth, electricity, energy. They take care of tasks for us. But we only do proper justice to this fact if we perform other tasks for which the achievements of nature and technology have liberated us.[20]

The age of the new Paradise on earth is the age not of threats, but of invitations. Each person is invited to eat as much fruit from the Tree of Knowledge as possible. Its fruits do not diminish when harvested; rather they become more abundant. That is the new Garden of Eden. The veil is lifted. Anyone who does not participate in it will have problems. With themselves. On a postcard by Joseph Beuys it says: "Anyone unwilling to think is fired (oneself)."[21]

The Russian Nobel Prize winner for economics, Wassily Leontief, formulates precisely the modern Paradise paradox: "The history of technological progress over the past 200 years is essentially the story of the human species working its way slowly and steadily back into Paradise. What would happen, however, if we suddenly found ourselves in it? With all goods and services provided without work, no one would be gainfully employed. Being unemployed means receiving no wages. As a result, until appropriate new income policies were formulated to fit the changed technological conditions, everyone would starve in Paradise."[22] Leontief sketches here the heavenly world on earth, in which those who receive no income suffer the torments of Hell.

Unconditional basic income grants everyone what they need and invites everyone to show what they are capable of. There is no shortage of products today. What we are short of if we are not to perish in the midst of our abundance is courage and imagination. These cannot be coerced; they can only be enabled.

People Unwilling to Work Are Sick

"If anyone would not work, neither should he eat." These words of St. Paul's are a component of our business contract. Whoever annuls it by refusing to work mustn't hope to receive financial support from our society. Social benefits provided by the government are reserved for people who despite proven effort or due to disability, youth or old age are unable, not yet able, or no longer able to engage in gainful employment. Indolence, i.e., the unwillingness to work, is considered a betrayal of this agreement.

The question that follows from this is: What reasons are there for a person's not wanting to work? German entrepreneur Götz W. Werner, founder of the leading European drugstore, response to this question drastically: "People unwilling to work are sick."[23]

The conventional opinion is: Anyone who is unwilling to work is evil. Such a person resists the moral expectation that we must work. But irrespective of the question of good or evil—it is beneath the dignity of a liberal society to revoke the foundation of a person's existence.

Our liberal society has meanwhile noticed that its apparently pleasing morality of gainful employment actually provokes unwillingness to work. Laziness is no anthropological constant; rather, it is a healthy reaction to activities which the immune system of our sense of meaning senses as meaningless, unworthy and unnecessary. Since we indulge nowadays in more and more activities of this kind, because indulgence have become an end in itself, we no longer have any capacity to focus on an activity's meaningfulness. In other words: Whoever thinks that there is nothing to do does best to leave all well alone.

This sets us up for a statement that complements Götz W. Werner's diagnosis: Anyone who works in a meaningless way is sick. Willingness to work as a hollow urge, as a conditioned mode of existence is pathological. Work needs to be done, is carried out, and fulfills those who perform it, as long as it is meaningful. A false passion for work improves the world for the worse.

In the course of reaching our objective, we often lose sight of it. German philosopher Hannah Arendt reveals this phenomenon in her main work *The Human Condition*. According to Arendt, the labor-centered society fights for a survival which has long been guaranteed with no need of struggle. Over the years, labor-centered society has forgotten that it works not for work's sake, but for the sake of leisure, and now of all times, just when *homo faber* would no longer have to toil from dawn to dusk, the ability to do anything else has been lost: "It is a society of laborers which is about to be liberated from the fetters of labor, and this society does no longer know of those other higher and more meaningful activities for the sake of which this freedom would deserve to be won. [...] What we are confronted with is the prospect of a society of laborers without labor, that is, without the only activity left to them. Surely, nothing could be worse."[24]

Instead of working for leisure and liberty, we are working ourselves to death. We are not hardworking to the point of abundance, but rather to the point of nausea. This would not have to happen if our labor-centered society were to succeed in finding a basic income consisting not in the idealization of gainful employment, but rather in the realization of possibilities for freedom that are just waiting to come about.

Machines Function, Humans Act

Whoever sees a task that needs doing does well in doing it. The purpose of work is not to be guaranteed, but to be carried out. As efficiently as possible. As intelligently as possible. This holds for all activities that people perform, and for as long as it takes to invent a machine that can carry out the task in a manner more efficient than the people themselves can. The dirty work is the job a person has to do even though a machine could do it. What makes the work dirty is that someone makes us do it even though there is nothing left for us to do. Meaningful work is never dirty work.

Alongside mechanical and monotonous activities that in the future will increasingly be taken over by machines, there are also activities that above all require devotion on the part of human beings. Beethoven's Ninth Symphony cannot be played efficiently any more than children in schools can be taught or grandparents cared for efficiently. What matters is not playing as many notes in as short a time as possible, or teaching as many children with as little inclination from the teacher as possible, or tending to our grandparents with as little care as possible; rather, what matters here is simply that what is dictated by the very human encounter itself be allowed to come about. For the music's sake. For the children's sake. For the grandparents' sake.

Machines function, humans act. Service by the book calls for commands, thinking requires spare time, along with institutions for human research: kindergartens, schools, academies. It is not the hardworking thinker who has new ideas. Only when my view is free and my thoughts can roam in a leisurely way can new ideas occur to me. The law of gravity was not discovered by someone standing on a ladder diligently picking apples, but rather by the one observing how an apple never falls far from the tree and in accordance with a certain law. The automobile was not invented by searching for better horses. It took mobility of thought, a reframing of the question, a good idea.

Microsoft founder Bill Gates, Amazon founder Jeff Bezos, Wikipedia founder Jimmy Wales, Facebook founder Mark Zuckerberg and Google founders Larry Page and Sergey Brin all went to Montessori Schools.[25] All of them have changed the world because they later took their time and tinkered around with what they thought belonged to the future. Today we consider Microsoft, Amazon, Wikipedia, Facebook and Google part of our everyday life; but not the way they came about, which was not pure drudgery, but at their leisure—out of their free time and free will.

Unconditional basic income keeps us from stifling the invention of time-saving machines simply because tasks that need doing guarantee income-producing jobs. Basic income makes it possible for machines to take care of everything they command. And for us it makes leisure possible, which is the sole measure of human interaction.

Basic income leads neither to a dictatorship of hard work nor to one of indolence. Whereas in our times the two are played against each other because we demand hard work but promote laziness—through refraining from more efficient production—basic income enables the leisure that first provides the foundation for hard work.

No pain, no gain? The gain of basic income is that only what we truly want becomes successful. It makes space for us to develop our own will—because it deprives external demands of the power to come between ourselves and our own activity. Basic income doesn't make it easier to will, but it does make non-willing more visible. Today we grant considerable support to non-willing. Unconditional basic income brings that to an end. It flushes out non-willing and by exposing it brings in honesty. And it promises commitment. If I do what I want, I am more committed than I could ever be otherwise.

I'm Busy, You're Lazy

One statement that crystalizes innumerable misunderstandings and prejudices, assertions and allegations, is: I'm busy, you're lazy. At first glance, this claim seems harmless. Of course: I am hardworking. I apply myself. I get involved. And the others? They too might be a little hardworking, if you force them to be—but as rule they tend to be less hardworking than I am. Of course: No pain, no gain; no stress, no success; no work, no wealth; laziness, indolence, listlessness will ruin us yet! Of course: The hardworking take care of themselves, pay their own way, stand up for themselves—while the lazybones live at others' expense. They swing their life away in the social hammock thanks to the hardworker's moxie.

So far, so rash. After all, what is really at the root of diligence and laziness? And the connection between me and you? And work done by humans, which runs along a continuum between the concepts of diligence (working hard) and laziness (refusing to work)? What gain does laziness promise? What tragedy inheres in diligence? What task does the work determine? And last but not least: What meaning does the way we think about each other have?

Let's look first at the ancient Germanic origin of the present day German word for diligence: *Fleiß*. *Fleiß* meant fighting spirit, even belligerence, before it came to designate the civil virtue of industrious and obedient goal orientedness. In Greek antiquity, by contrast, this trait was frowned upon. That was what slaves were for. Only the leisurely reached the Muses, and successful politics could only come about out of leisure. Today, the opposite seems to hold: Whoever is not industrious earns nothing. Instead of relying on the Muses or the gods, hardworking people rely on themselves or their superiors.

Anyone wishing to rely on themselves in a society built around divided labor has truly taken leave of their senses. No one works for themselves anymore, the hardest working people least of all. All of us have long since worked for others, for each other. The reality of the division of labor consists in my receiving from others and in my giving to others. Whether this gift is most effective when I am hardworking is questionable. Anyone hardworking turns into a machine. They automatize themselves. The automatized human being is neither effective nor innovative. Hardworking machines—the "slaves" of modern times—are invented not by the hardworking, but by the idle. That is the law of innovation: no idleness, no industriousness. We owe our gain to idleness.

And laziness? If by laziness we mean slothfulness of the heart, then we are talking about one of Christianity's seven deadly sins: *acedia*. It has nothing to do with meditation and deepening, with reverence and mindfulness, leisure and contemplation. On the contrary: The lazy sinner renounces a life in God—later in history, a working life. The frivolousness the lazy person formerly committed against God he now commits against his fellow human beings, as he is only capable of living off them because they are different from him, that is, they are hardworking.

On the other hand, every fruit must first rot before, with its seed's help, it can ripen again. Unlike the laziness that denies its own ideals and other peoples' expectations, the laziness that prepares the new serves the future. It is not a sin; rather, it is one of the reasons why new things can come into the world.

I'm busy, you're lazy. This utterance reveals the fact that something is lazy or even rotten in assiduous thinkers. For we claim diligence for ourselves and laziness for the others. We cultivate a split image of the human being: a subhuman image of the others and a superhuman image of ourselves. Basic income challenges me to rethink my notion of myself and of others. For as long as I think of others as if they were inhabitants of a zoo, I will consider them to be sloths in need of proper motivation. If, however, I can manage to regard others as different people, then it is possible for us to live together in a way that relies on the power of courage and leisure beyond diligence and laziness.

Working Losers and Champions of Free Time

TGI Friday's is not just a successful American fast food chain. TGIF is the well-known acronym for "Thank God It's Friday." What does it mean that we look forward to Friday in this way? What is it that we want to be free of or free for on Fridays?

Anyone who does something they do not want to do for eight hours is pretty exhausted at the end of it—and likely during, as well. Starting Monday morning, they long for Friday evening. Finishing work for the day, the weekend, vacation: These are the highlights for people unable to identify with their jobs in the right way.

Am I still working, or have I started to live? Whoever works for eight hours—nine to five—with no passion for performance works for a life beyond working life. Work is more or less of secondary importance. The most important thing are our hobbies. During our free time we are fully occupied. The main objective is recovering from work by means of wellness activities, jogging, shopping and partying. It's quite understandable that we become more and more stressed in the process. What is the consequence? Recovering from our recovery. Our workplace becomes the place where we sleep.

We live in a work-centered society that finds its fulfillment as an amusement society. We pursue our free-time activities in a downright compulsive way. Amusement offers sprout out of the ground like mushrooms after a warm autumn rain. And what do we do at work in such a stressed state of mind? We plan and book our free-time activities. The easy jet-setters burn their energy drinking Red Bull on weekend trips to Berlin or Barcelona. It gives us wings. In the short run. But it's no use: In the end we find ourselves bored again. We are the working losers and the champions of free time.

Rather than building up new perspectives, we dumb down in amusement parks and shopping centers. Why? Because not enough is demanded of us at the workplace—not in the sense that people count on us and that what we do is important.

Monday stands for hangover. Tuesday stands for performance by the book. Wednesday for evaluation conferences. Thursday we need to get by—and then the goal is almost there: Friday. Saturday is the day after Friday and Sunday the day of mourning: Monday is approaching.

The other phenomenon looks like this: Our best time we spend on the job. Thank God It's Monday. We get to return to our workplace, where we have free space. In our free time we often feel pressured to do things, to be athletic, to have fun. In our free time and especially at the weekend we are exposed to the demands of our friends. They all want something from us. There's no place for us to hide. During the week we can go underground at the office—wonderful.

Common to both these phenomena is that we don't enjoy our work. First it's coercion, in the end it's escape. Why aren't we glad to work? Because we've been taught that we have to work! What you have to do you don't do with pleasure. Therefore, it's very unwise to perpetuate coercion.

We have outsourced our free will to the amusement sector. And since we are under pressure to feel free in our free time we have become stressed. Our free will dissipates because we are expected to be free. Work, by contrast, feels unfree because we think that others think that we have to work.

The result: The hammocks hang in the offices, not in the vacation homes. And in the vacation homes there are desks. What does that mean? That means that we are always unhappy with what we are doing, as long as we are not doing what we really want.

What Motivates Us?

When someone has a good idea, it can motivate me to become active. That works best when I can make the idea my own. This is not taking the other person's idea away from them; it's just sharing it. Communicating it. Through the act of sharing, the idea does not get smaller; rather, it grows.

If I am supposed to follow through on someone else's idea but am unable to make it my own, I have no enthusiasm. I motivate myself differently. By means of money, for instance. Or I say to myself: so what? I don't think the work is important, but I meet interesting people there. Or: I don't find the work particularly interesting, but that co-worker is attractive. If you don't really want to do something you have to find something else to motivate you. In matters of motivation, the difference between having and wanting to do something comes to direct expression. Wanting to do something has a motivating effect, having to do something has a crippling one.

And what about incentives? Countless studies have been conducted on the subject. Best-selling American author Daniel H. Pink delivers a concise summary of what truly motivates us in his book *Drive*. With mechanistic activities requiring little or no human intelligence, monetary incentives function quite well. But the moment demands are made on our thinking, monetary incentives lead to inferior performance. Human beings cannot be motivated by means of money to perform better. In fact, the inverse holds. The moment the human being enters the picture as a human being, non-monetary values are what counts. Whoever tries to lure using money, lures displeasure and hampers innovation.[26]

The biggest motivation killers, says Pink, are lack of appreciation, patronizing, reward and punishment, lack of information, non-transparency, unfair treatment, control and surveillance, distrustful bosses and supervisors, false praise, unfounded criticism, failure, and lack of acknowledgement. What promotes motivation are appreciation, respect, transparency, trust, self-responsibility, acknowledgement and curiosity, as well as all the variant forms of spurring challenge. Why do people watch so many crime series? Why do they do millions of crossword puzzles and Sudoku's every day? It is motivating to find things out, to take things in hand, to help people, to be able to surprise people. Anyone taking part in this way does so with joy.

Each year on a certain day in Israel, school children go from house to house to collect donations for charitable causes. On one such day, Uri Gneezy and Aldo Rustichini, two American behavioral economists, had three different test groups of children set out. The one group was simply told how important their job was for society, a second group was also promised a commission of one per cent on all the donations they collected; a third group was promised ten per cent of the total donations. By the end of the day those school children who had been promised the larger commission had collected considerably more than the ones promised only one per cent. But the most successful children were those with no prospect of financial compensation.[27]

This study is not the only one to demonstrate how a person's own inner motivation can be and frequently is suppressed or displaced by means of external incentives. Besides this so-called crowding-out effect, they brought a further insight to light. They asked the participants in their experiment how they would seek to incent other people to collect money: offer them no financial compensation, one per cent, or ten per cent of the total donations.

Almost all of them voted for a compensation of one per cent—that is, the amount that had proven to be the weakest motivator. This is the dilemma: When asked what motivates others, we almost always assume for others what neither applies to ourselves nor to them.

Competing Competitions

Competition in the area of existential necessity is out of place. Competition in the area of ideas, projects and products is exactly the right thing. Which idea is better? What looks better? What is more meaningful? Competition of ideas enlivens business; competition of existences endangers it.

Unconditional basic income enlivens the competition of ideas. With a financially guaranteed starting position that is in no way jeopardized—not even by one's strongest competitors—the competition can unfold more freely. If by engaging in competition I place others in existential need, I myself am hampered in my actions. If I am certain of my competitor's existential certainty, I am better able to compete. I am freer to engage in the contest. Of course I want to contend with everything I have, but not at the expense of other people's existential security.

It takes basic income for us to be able to get down to being enterprising without endangering other peoples' existence. That being said though, we are not talking here about the neoliberal, competitive use of elbows. This does not mean that if we have a basic income we no longer need to take care of others; it only means that we no longer need to pit competition against securing our livelihood and *vice versa*.

Basic income provides the basis to be able to take everyone seriously instead of taking pains to beat around the bush concerning projects and goals, which are frequently watered down by the need for an income. Today we again and again have to hold back and mind that we do not endanger anyone's livelihood, even when we think what they are doing is total nonsense. I cannot really hold anyone accountable for their actions as long as I know they have to earn an income so they can feed their family.

Unconditional basic income grants us free expression of our agreement and criticism without automatically bringing the question of income into play. If the other person's basic income is guaranteed, then I can arouse their passion on the subject at hand, or I can challenge them or even provoke them. Often situations occur in which there are plenty of good ideas and work could begin—but the income problem holds everything up!

The competition of ideas established by this new deal expands the possible forms that competition can take. A subtler form of competition is cooperation. I work together with others who support and challenge me. Competition as survival of the fittest is fatal, as it does not presuppose the other person's survival as self-evident. If the person with whom I wish to interact is engaged in a constant struggle for survival, they are not engaging with me as a partner. But the only existences I can count on for interaction are ones that are actually there and present, standing opposite me. Basic income makes it possible for people to be competitors and cooperative partners at the same time.

On Pressure that Turns into Suction

When something pinches or squeezes or rubs because it no longer fits, a change is called for—either we ourselves must change, or the thing that pinches, squeezes or rubs must be changed. Pressure is the experience that something can no longer stay the way it is. This is not a bad thing in itself. What can be bad is the influence pressure exert, namely when it cuts us off from just those opportunities we would need to seek out. This pressure changes into coercion. And coercion is crippling. It does not liberate; it does not alter. It rigidifies and stiffens us.

The pressure created by taking on a social obligation can release unforeseen powers. A project to be presented, a manuscript to be submitted, can spur us to peak performance the same way that the impending arrival of guests or an upcoming voting campaign can. What these situations have in common is the liberty to place oneself within them. As long as I am aware that the pressure is something I have chosen because I want to challenge myself in some way, it inspires me. If I lose this awareness or never had it in the first place—maybe because I'm studying what my parents want me to or because I feel obligated to come up with a gift for someone—then these situations will also feel oppressive.

Our current understanding of pressure assumes that that existential pressure motivates us to peak performance. The tenor of this notion is that in the face of an existentially precarious situation I would try almost anything to avert an impending loss. If there is any truth at all in this thought, it is a cruel truth: Whoever sees their existence at risk changes from a human being into an animal. They are broken as a human being because their humanity is no longer taken into consideration; rather, their existence is at stake. Hence existential pressure hampers creativity, involvement, innovation, health, and social competency. Obviously, people under pressure are capable of hard work—and they grease the wheel of the rat race. But such meaningless work is ill-suited to a society direly threated by its own abundance.

There is constructive pressure, and there is destructive pressure. Fear for one's existence is almost always destructive. Pressure usually exerts a positive influence when it becomes suction. When it inspires us. When it becomes wind beneath our wings so we can lift off; so that initiative can be successful; so that we have the courage to bring about change in the world in matters close to our heart.

Existential pressure does not stimulate; rather, it oppresses. It weighs down on us. In division of labor we rely on others being inspired, in order for them to be active for us in the best way. Basic income is an advance on initiative. It does not consider today's unemployment to be a problem; instead, it considers today's lack of income to be a threat to people's existence and to have a crippling effect on initiative. This is why basic income diminishes the pressure that hinders us and promotes the pressure that inspires us. It's about us being able to set each other on fire—through the obligations we have toward one another, and not the sanctions we impose on each other.

Pleasure or Frustration?
On Entrepreneurship

With basic income we will be more active and more independent. That could be a disadvantage for companies that profit from their employees' dependence on income. In the low-wage sector, for example, the quota of people who refuse job offers would probably rise. The deciding factor for business enterprises will be how well their workers can identify with the enterprise's purpose and with the way it cultivates entrepreneurship. Basic income strengthens workers against businesses that treat them poorly. And it strengthens businesses in the certainty that their employees will work in the spirit of the undertaking's purpose and in their own personal interest rather than for simply earning an income. Business ventures can then be more flexible, as they no longer have to lay anyone off due to lack of revenues. And we ourselves can be more flexible, because fear for our own livelihood no longer makes us hang on to a job that we don't like or is unfulfilling.

For people who already are or wish to be self-employed, the basic income they receive can function as start-up capital. Start-ups could shoot up out of the ground. If my own livelihood is guaranteed, I can participate much better in everything I really want to do. Today many initiatives simply lie fallow due to the shear struggle to survive. Any organization with a meaningful mission but not enough money would profit from the implementation of basic income.

People with a basic income can no longer say, "I would really like to, but my hands are tied." With basic income, our impetus goes into the actual work, into how something could actually function. The impetus would no longer be wasted in looking for reasons why something can't work. The selling power of an idea would take center stage and the sway held by money would recede into the background. To someone who is existentially insecure, money talks louder than good ideas. Someone who stands on a solid financial basis is better able to take note and act. Anyone who cannot afford to say "no" is, by the same token, only capable of a weak "yes." It is important to imagine how much more productively and efficiently we could manage our finances if our frustration were to diminish and our pleasure to rise. People who do things with joy are more effective.

Happiness arises above all when we can take hold of and determine our own work. A survey conducted by Swiss economists Matthias Benz and Bruno S. Frey shows that on average in Switzerland the self-employed report a greater satisfaction with their work than salaried employees. This can also be observed in Germany and the USA, as well as Japan or Bangladesh. Indeed, the survey yielded the same finding in all 23 of the countries that participated.[28]

Benz's and Frey's study furthermore illustrates that the high degree of work satisfaction on the part of the self-employed is attributable to two decisive factors: their greater autonomy and a more strongly felt interest in the activities they pursue. The more individualistic Western society is not the only one that appreciates autonomy and interesting work. In Japan as well people who are self-employed are more satisfied with their work than salaried employees—even though it is widely assumed that people in the allegedly collectivist societies of Asia feel themselves especially well taken care of in an organization. Thus the independence of the self-employed proves to be a source of job satisfaction in the Far East as well. Basic income democratizes this source of satisfaction by enabling everyone to draw from it.

Laziness I

Nothing stands more in the way of unconditional basic income than the fact that people are lazy by nature. Once the monthly income a person needs reaches their bank account, laziness takes root, sprouts branches and blossoms. The fruits of the tree of laziness, though, are toxic. They destroy solidarity and morale. The economy will collapse and there will no longer be any basic income.

We need resistance; otherwise a vacuum is created. We need something that spurs us on, an incentive. Without challenges we fall short of our potential. This is why we make appointments, set ourselves goals, make and keep agreements. We obligate ourselves. This has nothing to do with coercion or heteronomy. Rather, it has to do with commitment and responsibility.

Those in favor of unconditional basic income point to the allegedly missing possibility of saying "no." But is there anything at all these days we could not say "no" to, provided we spare no effort and are prepared to bear the consequences? Freedom does not mean not having to do anything. Freedom is strenuous and does not come about by receiving an income for doing nothing. If freedom were something money could buy, it would not be worth mentioning; rather, it would be a consumer good, like toothpaste. Freedom does not mean that everyone has it unconditionally. Freedom is the fruit of achievement. Freedom cannot be had simply by making it rain money.

The human being is a complex entity. The fact that humans must work is not inhuman. By working they develop and evolve. Our problem is that work is again and again condemned as evil. However, it is fulfilling. It endows our existence with meaning and integrates us into society. Unconditional basic income seeks under the pretense of freedom to do away with work. But it destroys people instead. It deprives them of the resistance that makes life worth living in the first place. It promises false freedom that makes them become slack and mediocre.

Unconditional basic income resembles the creeping disarmament of the self-responsible adult. It postulates liberty and creates loneliness. Moreover, it divides the population into people who are free and people who only appear free. It wants to grant humanity a foundation for its free development. But a monthly blank check for doing nothing causes the exact opposite: To be sure, with money one can buy goods and services, but the free unfolding of the human personality is something money can't buy. Getting something for nothing is precisely what freedom does not mean. Unconditional basic income is ill-considered. If no one has to do anything anymore, no one will be able to. This is the beginning of the end.

Laziness II

Nothing stands more in the way of unconditional basic income than the prejudice that people are lazy by nature. They are not. The laziness prejudice is an anthropological conspiracy theory. People want to be self-determined. They want to work, to get involved, to help others. No one wants to just lie around in a hammock for no good reason.

Why do people become lazy? Why do people become hard-working? When we want to do something we have the greatest strength at our disposal. It is not motivating at all to have to do something when we can't see the point of it. It is highly motivating to do something for a good reason. Does the business I work for pursue goals that I support? If yes, I am willing to do a great deal. If not, I require motivation from a different source. That can be my salary or my reputation. In either case, the motivation for my work is external to the work itself.

Unconditional basic income protects work from external motivation, and it protects us from becoming lazy. The paradigm change unconditional basic income rings in is: First comes income, then pleasure. Income is the basis for free motivation. Independent motives turn work into pleasure. External motives are long-term motivation killers. Freedom can be neither bought nor earned. It can only be enabled or prevented. It is liberating to renounce denying other people's freedom.

Work seeks income. No income, no work. Income is not the fruit we work for; rather, it is the seed out of which work grows. Income does not grow like apples on trees. Income puts us in a position to plant trees and harvest apples. Therefore, the motivation to doing work lies within the very work itself.

If we have to do something that not only does not motivate us, but actually puts us off, we develop an attitude of defiance. Why should I feel a passion for doing something that I find neither meaningful nor useful? If such a situation continues long enough, we become lazy. Laziness is the rebellion against the concrete existence of meaninglessness.

Laziness is a disease. It occurs as a purging fever when people do the wrong thing for a long time. Thus it founds the possibility of doing the right thing in the future. This is the beginning of a new beginning.

False Friends: Deceptive Alternatives

Seductions are distractions. Distractions from what really matters. Not productive distractions, but destructive ones. The techniques of distraction are manifold. The cause of our downfall could be false promises or false goals: If you meet this or that target or clear this or that bar, then you've made it. But in this case what we don't notice is not that we want to meet the wrong target or clear the wrong bar, but that it is completely wrong to think in terms of targets to meet or bars to clear.

Deceptive alternatives are one particular form of seduction. They pit against each other what depends on each other. But the opposite of a deceptive alternative is just as wrong. More than wrong. Being the opposite of what's wrong doesn't make it right. The two are false friends. By thinking that what we are doing is right, we miss what is right by an even wider margin. "Money is of no importance whatsoever," say the ones—and fill their already full pockets even fuller with lies. "Money is the only thing that counts," say the others—and do not make things any better simply because they don't have any. It does justice neither to money nor to oneself either to glorify it or to scorn it.

We rescue ourselves from deceptive alternatives by flushing them out and revealing a third alternative. "Man does not live by bread alone," as it says in the Gospel according to St. Matthew.[29] This does not mean: Man does not live by bread at all (deceptive alternative 1). Nor does it mean: Man lives by bread alone (deceptive 2). It means someone does not live only by bread—that is, that they live by both bread and the word that goes "forth from the mouth of God."

Whoever thinks basic income is unnecessary because money is not the most important thing in life (deceptive alternative 1), is on just as wrong a path as someone who thinks that with basic income they have finally attained the ultimate goal—that is, more money in the bank (deceptive alternative 2). No: Unconditional basic income is the basis for going beyond it—and to go beyond it we need basic income. Its basis is that something else can become the basis for its existence—the human being for whom it exists.

Which deceptive alternative victimizes us today? The concept of work can certainly be counted among them: We give work top priority and threaten everyone else who does not appear as if they have it or are after it (deceptive alternative 1), but at the same time we think negatively about work—namely, that working time is for doing what we don't want so that afterwards we can do what we do want (deceptive alternative 2).

Unconditional basic income lets us take up the work that we think is meaningful without leaving the work that needs to get done unfinished. It does not disqualify working time as inferior life time—nor does it fetishize work as the only form of human acknowledgement there is. Basic income liberates labor so that we can take it up in freedom. It exposes the deceptive alternatives that hinder our doing so.

From Leadership to Self-Leadership

People unable to identify with the things they do are in danger of becoming lazy. Does this mean that with unconditional basic income lazy people would become even lazier? No. The first thing that would happen is that they would go through a phase of sobering up. Basic income means no longer having to do what one doesn't want to do. So is there a cure for laziness? Yes. And what would this cure be? Doing what one wants to do.

Unconditional basic income is a disciplinary measure for making one's own way in life. Children have a natural command over this discipline. They would never not do what they want to do. Children also have the opposite skill at their command: They would never do what they didn't want to do. The older children get, the more they are made to rid themselves of this self-discipline. Grown-ups discipline them. External discipline.

Why? Because of the know-it-alls. Because of people who think they know better what is right for other people. Because of the leaders. But the only legitimate leadership for the future will be guidance toward self-leadership. On this topic, German philosopher Karl-Martin Dietz writes that, "in our times, in which individualization is so predominant, the individual is responsible for the modes of his actions to an extent unknown in the past. He is less and less able to prop himself up on stable traditions, and increasingly forced to design his own life. That calls for the will and the skills we need to guide ourselves, and it places new demands on collaboration between people who in this way have become individualized."[30]

In the future, people who don't learn to lead themselves will become isolated. And then they actually will need leadership, because they will be unable to lead themselves. But people who need to be led do not determine the direction. They become directed.

With unconditional basic income, we don't give up on those who indulge in self-neglect. We give up trying to make different people out of them from the ones they want to make of themselves. Today they are discounted because they don't do what we want. That's why we take care of them. Not because we care for them, but because they don't follow us.

Categorizing people as in need of help and treating them accordingly is the most promising way of keeping them from doing what they want. The logic behind this is: Those in need of my help must do what I want. All I need to do is show them they are inept for as long as it takes them to believe they really are. Then I can help them. Then they are willing for me to help them.

The most efficient method of making people helpless is to deny their abilities and then keeps them on a short leash. People who are kept on a short leash and properly rewarded can be led and molded best. The more dependent someone is, the less they determine themselves. The most dependent dependency is dependency on existential security. People who fear for their existence are the easiest to manipulate. This is well-known fact from the practice of torture. To deny people their self-discipline is also a form of torture, albeit a rather subtle one.

"You must work; otherwise you will die," we whisper into the ears of those unwilling and unable to work. That is wrong. What is right is: You must work; otherwise your fellow human beings will die. People who understand this are concerned for the well-being of the others, on whom alone their own well-being depends.

The Liberation of Work

Unconditional basic income unites what is social with what is liberal. It is liberal because it is unconditional and it is social because it is for everyone. It makes social what is liberal (the opposite of neoliberal) and it makes liberal what is social (the opposite of socialistic).

These two ideals have been contending with each other for ages: freedom or justice? The political left fights with the political right, labor fights with capital. It is a seemingly irresolvable antagonism, one that cements our political and our economic situation. But basic income dissolves this antagonism. Not as a party of the new center, but rather as an idea that leads away from the parties —which are partial—and toward the individual human being.

Work is a human affair. But work is weighed down by a curse. During World War II a sign was mounted above the entry gate to the concentration camp in Auschwitz. This sign displayed the words *Arbeit macht frei*—"labor liberates." Work and liberty were misused as ciphers for coercion and destruction. "Labor liberates" was written on the sign; *Vernichtung durch Arbeit*— "destruction through work" was in fact the Nazi doctrine.[31]

Countless people were forced to dig their own graves in the concentration camps. Millions died. It is important both to remember them and to be certain of the cynicism of utilizing the concepts of work and freedom for the most inhumane of actions.

The death camps were closed down seven decades ago. The abuse of the concept of work still goes on. And so we need to liberate the concept of work, which even today takes humanity prisoner. Basic income organizes the liberation of work. It is no longer coercion, front line duty, dirty work. Work is what I want to do. Work is the area in which I wish to undertake my own self-development. Work is what gives me strength and meaning. In work I sense myself as a whole human being.

Working is human. There's something wrong with anyone unwilling to work. But there's also something wrong with a society where everyone has to work. Work makes us free as long as liberty is its precondition. Unconditional basic income frees us to liberate work.

All Those Opposed

Assault on Human Dignity

"For me it is an assault on human dignity if a person receives an ill-considered unconditional basic income. It is a fundamental contradiction of my idea of social values. A society lives from knowledge on the part of every single one of its members that they must make a contribution. [...] Earning a living for oneself is the core of self-responsibility, the core of a life in freedom. [...] Basic income is the antithesis of freedom. It creates a society of people dependent on the state. It is a planned economy, a socialistic method. [...] It would ultimately destroy Switzerland."[32]

Roger Köppel, journalist

No Right to Basic Income

"No one in a liberal state is entitled to income. But there is an entitlement to liberty, understood especially as freedom from coercion by the state. [...] Those concerned with upholding the welfare state should not put forward any utopian and freedom-depriving ideas such as unconditional basic income. On the contrary: People ought to be granted more freedom to secure themselves on their own responsibility against risks to their livelihood."[33]

Michael Schoenenberger, journalist

Motivation Killer for the Youth

"I would not like our children or our children's children to be born in a society in which the government turned everyone into a life-long professional retiree. The promise of a constant government pension would become a motivation and energy killer for many young people; not for all of them, to be sure; but it would be a social incentive for a fundamental no-get-up-and-go attitude that leads to lost chances in life."[34]

Rudolf Strahm, politician

Making Junkies of the Entire Population

"The instrument of an unconditional basic income [...] is an assault on the very heart of our system today, in so far as it carries self-responsibility to the point of absurdity and establishes an intravenous connection between the individual and the state. [...] This system is in fact against nature. The state says here's enough money for you. You can go work if you want to. But you don't have to. That leads to a sluggish society and makes junkies out of an entire population. [...] People become idle and lazy if you just set everything in front of them."[35]

Philipp Müller, politician

Exploited by Slackers

"This makes us all unable to protect ourselves from exploitation by people unwilling to fend for themselves despite being able to. An unconditional basic income means no more and no less than 'freedom for everyone, responsibility for everyone except me'. That can't work. [...] Look at it any way you like. Unconditional basic income is an idea that not only aims wide of social and human reality, but jars at our very foundations."[36]

Katja Gentinetta, consultant

Permanent Vacation

"Basic income would be an immense and unbelievable government intervention. It would without fail lead to our marginalization. [...] Unconditional basic income liberates—but only those unwilling to work. Those who continue working would be crushed by the tax burden. [...] Parents with three or four children could actually go on permanent vacation if each family member received a basic income."[37]

Reiner Eichenberger, economist

Much too Expensive and for the Rich

"I am against an unconditional basic income, and not just because it would be too expensive, but because it would have to be paid to every single citizen. If a young man with rich parents didn't want to work, he would get an unconditional basic income all the same, in order to take care of himself in all respects. Other people have to work for this, people toward whom he demonstrates no solidarity."[38]

Gregor Gysi, politician

Scorn for Work Effort

"Once again, a reheating of the well-known free lunch incapable of economic existence. [...] With basic security, a lot of low-income consumers would give up working: immigrants, career entrants, part-time workers, single parents, married women who contribute to the family income. Labor participation would experience a dramatic drop. [...] Today, more than half of all households in Western Europe receive a portion of their income from the government. [...] The centralization of society is already highly advanced, and basic income would make it totalitarian. [...] The few left who would be willing to earn money by working would be outvoted. [...] There really is nothing thought through, nothing calculated, nothing liberal, nothing social behind it."[39]

Beat Kappeler, journalist

From Citizens to Government Slaves

"The new popular initiative for an unconditional basic income promises us all a better life. It is, after all, far more pleasant to pass around and eat cake at midday than it is to get up at four in the morning and bake cake for others. [...] Unfortunately, this liberation turns out in reality to be a penitentiary of government stable feeding. A collective of state retirees. Citizens who have been turned into government slaves. It's a shame that someone would also have to pay for the redistribution system, and that it would have to be paid for by means of forced financing in which some of the citizens would have to pay for the other citizens. [...] For many people in the world, though, our land would become a paradise to which they simply must immigrate. With an unconditional basic income [...] we would all soon be equal; that is, everyone would be poor."[40]

Christoph Mörgeli, politician

People Cannot Be Changed

"A paycheck at the end of the month is more than a mere money transfer. People who lose their jobs learn in an especially painful way how important money is as an expression of acknowledgement for work done. For a lot of people, work is more than just a way of passing the time. To be sure, nearly all of us wish for more free time, but once we have it, it can become a problem. Some are plunged into a crisis of values and meaning after a mere two weeks of vacation. [...] One might find it pitiful that work and wages are so important to us. But we just happen by cultural circumstance to be a work-centered society. [...] A lot of people would be ill-served if someone sought to change them by means of a guaranteed basic income."[41]

Patrick Feuz, journalist

Abolishing the Force of Gravity

"'Those who work pay for those unable to.' The popular initiative wants to turn the principle into: 'Those who want to work pay for those unwilling to.' [...] A person needn't exactly be 'lazy' to find a certain form of gainful employment less attractive under these circumstances. One need only be able to do arithmetic. [...] In reality, the popular initiative for basic income [...] would be like a popular initiative to do away with the force of gravity."[42]

Hansueli Schöchli, journalist

The System Will Collapse

"A lot of people would likely no longer have any incentive to pursue gainful employment; younger people couldn't see any sense in applying themselves in school or at their vocational training—and why should they? The state provides for their livelihood. But before the cake is passed around, it first has to be baked. And if it gets smaller and smaller, the standard of living sinks. In the worst case the system collapses. The only positive aspect is the public debate on streamlining our much too complicated system of social benefits and taxes."[43]

Daniel Kalt, economist

Money Cannot just be Printed

"There must be no right to an income without gainful employment. Anything else would be punishing all those people who make an effort for their own income. [...] The money we receive as wages does not just come from the printer's; it much rather comes from our added value. [...] An unconditional basic income presupposes that people other than me generate added value on my behalf: If everybody thinks like this, who will be left to do all the work?"[44]

Daniela Schneeberger, politician

Symptom of Decadent Affluence

"The bill is no antidote against widespread poverty; rather, it is a symptom of affluence in a state of decay. It would not solve a single problem; only create myriads of new ones. [...] Unconditional basic income in the form in which it will be presented for popular vote is suicidal, irresponsible, recklessness at the level of national economy. Even more dubious in the end is the corruption of the concept behind it. [...] Doing away with responsibility for oneself also does away with individual freedom. And a more encompassing sense of responsibility for society as a whole can only be developed by independent and mature citizens, not by debased, unmotivated parasites."[45]

Manfred Rösch, journalist

Support for the System

"I believe that with the establishment of unconditional basic income people would accept the disengagement of a portion of our society from their right to work. [...] This would not be freeing these people; it would not be emancipating them. [...] We need to fight for a new definition of gainful employment. We need to fight for adequate compensation of unpaid child care and care of the elderly. [...] Basic income stabilizes the system. It paralyzes the consumer. The social differences we combat with all our strength remain."[46]

Corrado Pardini, politician

Hush Money for Losers

"The efforts to distinguish people unable to work from those unwilling to work [...] might not always succeed, but giving up such efforts [...] would amount to a declaration of bankruptcy on the part of enlightened government. Seen in this way, one could even go so far as to call unconditional basic income a way of rewarding losers on the job market for not opening their mouths: A government incapable of establishing conditions under which all its citizens could actually find work who are willing to provide for their own livelihood by means of gainful employment, [...] such a government would no longer need to deal with the losers yielded by its political failure; they would only need to provide these losers with 2500 Swiss Franks per month to keep them quiet."[47]

Lukas Rühli, economist

Enticement of the Promised Land

"The charm of the idea of a basic income is that of a land of milk and honey. Unconditional also means without effort. The money flutters into my house with no effort whatsoever. [...] The enormous seduction here is in thinking that a land of milk and honey would make people free and thus unleash their creativity. The opposite is the case. A land of milk and honey makes people indolent. It smothers creativity and imagination. It will bring human development and progress to a halt."[48]

Rainer Hank, journalist

Fear of Free Riders

"There is another thing, a central aspect of justice, that raises an objection to the so-called civil wage: the aspect of reciprocity. According to this objection, a person earns a wage not merely to qualify as a citizen, but first of all in order to make a contribution to society. The overall threat of social free riders increases where the gap diminishes between 'civil wages' and wages received in return for work performed. Even when work isn't done by the sweat of one's brow, it nevertheless demands an exertion that the someone or other prefers to avoid: The biographical investment that consists in timely acquisition of professional skills, along with a willingness to achieve, and last but not least professional, social and geographical mobility."[49]

Otfried Höffe, philosopher

Begetting Children as a Financial Strategy

"Many fend for themselves, are willing to do something, are willing to undertake some design in life. There are also a lot of people who enjoy having a hammock. I would not like to have a system in which, for all intents and purposes, the first are treated the same as the latter. Let's try to imagine: Two hammock-lovers, kind and likeable people, get together and draw 800 Euros each in basic income. Then they have ten children and receive another 8000 Euros in basic income. And then they live in joy and splendor on 9600 Euros. [...] We cannot pay people simply because they exist. It's not right."[50]

Thilo Sarrazin, politician

Threatened by Drone Existences

"It may, in terms of ethical justice, be reasonable for the collective to take care of someone unable to take care of themselves. But it cannot be ethically justified to permit a free choice between exempting oneself from work and engaging in work, without this choice being bound up with clear and definite consequences. [...] Basic income makes drone existences of citizens, makes them recipients without dignity and pride. It makes them unfree in the name of the greater good, in the name of 'real freedom'; it causes work ambition to be choked by the weeds of demand mentality. Everyone depends on the state, which functions as our *alma mater* and gives without receiving, even going without gratitude, as happens more and more with modern mothers."[51]

Wolfgang Kersting, philosopher

Dividing the Society

"The installation of an unconditional basic income would widen the already existing divide in our society between the vocationally integrated and those who, either through precarious and frequently changing occupational circumstance or unemployment, are not vocationally integrated. The implementation of an unconditional basic income would amount to giving up. Rather than following a strategy of integration and inclusion within a work-centered society, people would be financially rewarded for dropping out of this society entirely, which would then be irreversible."[52]

Julian Nida-Rümelin, philosopher

Shunning the Current Principles

"A system of unconditional basic income would call for a complete refinancing of social benefits. [...] That would be a rejection of the principle of demand on which our solidary welfare state has always been built, and which enables it to help when help is needed. Further, unconditional basic income would amount to a rejection of the principle of give and take on which both our unemployment insurance and our pension funding are based. But the federal government's purpose is to strengthen both the principle of demand and that of give and take. Inasmuch as this is the case, unconditional basic income is not on the government's current agenda."[53]

Angela Merkel, politician

Yielding to Capital

"Unconditional basic income withdraws capital from peoples' personal responsibility, because it is not the employer's job to disburse this means of guaranteeing people's existence, but the government's. The employer would only need to pay a possible increase. This would create the danger of employers exploiting basic income as a supplementary benefit in order to lower the actual wages they pay. It is likely a further reason for the large number of supporters of unconditional basic income in the employer camp."[54]

Sahra Wagenknecht, politician

In Contradiction to Human History

"I am against basic income because in the course of human history people have always had to be active in order to survive. I do not believe in an effortless income that rains down like manna from heaven. It promises income to those who do nothing. And it ignores the fact that it is precisely the working population that is expected to produce this basic income. This is pure nonsense, self-deception cubed."[55]

Oswald Metzger, politician

A Field Kitchen replaces the Welfare State

"This is yet another hit from the downright inexhaustible reformers' reservoir, brought to us by the people who want to do everything different. The civil pension is conceived of as a fixed amount of money that the government pays out to everybody. Everyone gets a ladle full from the field kitchen, which steps up to replace the welfare state. The civil pension is a uniform government wage. For some it will be a starvation wage, and for the others—i.e. the ones who have absolutely no need of it—it will be a gratuity. Whether a person is poor or rich: Before the civil pension everyone is equal. The civil pension is the steamroller that flattens the social state. The 'jobless' basic income, also known as citizens' income, is an infringement on everything we have ever learned about justice and solidarity. It measures everyone by the same yardstick. The age of leveling has begun."[56]

Norbert Blüm, politician

The Mind's Refusal to Work

"If you lose all contact with prevailing convictions—and one such conviction just happens to be the notion that there should only be money in return for real goods received and services performed—you also lose your credibility. Helicopter money, basic income, full-reserve banking and a number of other nice ideas are very enticing. You fly so high over the cuckoo's nest with them that you never bump into anyone, because no one takes you seriously. This spares you the daily grind and the tilting at intellectual windmills that make our life so hard."[57]

Heiner Flassbeck, economist

Who's the Boss when Everyone is the Boss?

Why the Popular Initiative is the Right Path

Unconditional basic income does not come from above. It is not a privilege granted by those on high; it is a fundamental right. First, fundamental rights had to be won in conflict with the powers that be. Once they had been won, the people had to grant them to each other.

As a fundamental right, basic income touches on the issue of power. It puts power more and more into the hands of the individual. The only effective way empowering the individual is through other individuals. The sovereign emancipated by basic income can only emancipate themselves.

In every one of the world's democracies except for Switzerland, the legislative body more or less monopolizes the actual legislative process. This is harmful to basic income. These legislative bodies can, of course, formally approve basic income at any time. But the fundamental gesture inherent in basic income is one of direct democracy. This gesture sets the relationship aright between citizens and politicians. Citizens are not supplicants who seek to sway the partiality of the politicians; rather, politicians are service providers who carry out the citizens' interests.

To be sure, dealing with specific issues of government finance is politicians' specialty. But only citizens can decide about fundamental rights. This is why the public initiative is the right path to launch unconditional basic income. This path is an object of worldwide admiration: Not only are the Swiss debating unconditional basic income, they are even taking a ballot on it. This is an accomplishment of direct democracy.

Beyond Party Politics

Nothing the political establishment prescribes is of any consequence for the constitutional referendum on unconditional basic income. In the everyday business of Swiss politics, the specifics of basic income cut a rather strange figure and are a frequent source of bafflement. This is shown by the message from the Swiss Federal Council and the deliberations in the panel of the National Council of Switzerland.[58] An almost grotesque sense of confoundment, bewilderment and awkwardness could be witnessed in the panel. Whether they come from the right wing or the left, the questions and objections raised by those in attendance were more or less an articulation of their incomprehension and in no way demonstrated that they had come to terms with the topic in any depth. No reproach intended here; it merely serves to show that the bill on basic income is one whose depths have yet to be plumbed in the everyday business of politics.

The Swiss political parties will recommend that basic income be rejected; their arguments will be its infinancibility, the unforseeability of its consequences, and concern over the loss of work incentives. Moreover, they will say that basic income is unsocial and bears the mark of neoliberalism, or that it is illiberal and bears the mark of socialism. The opponents' campaign posters will show slogans accordingly: "Money for nothing? Not if we can help it!"; "Yes to Switzerland! No to welfare parasites!"; "Freedom is not for free."

Basic income's questions are directed at each individual person. Political trench-fighting is marginal. Anyone who votes according to what others say instead of making basic income's questions their own is passing up an opportunity to ask themselves how they wish to live in the future.

What do we do when we no longer have to work? This is what the sociologist asks. What do we do when everyone else works for us? This is what the economist asks. The neighbor, the envier, the nihilist asks: Would anyone continue to work at all if their income were taken care of? The pessimist asks: And who's going to do all the dirty work? The conservative asks: Wouldn't all the foreigners come then? The philosopher asks: What is work, anyway? And the educator asks: Shouldn't we place conditions on unconditional basic income after all? Unconditional basic income inquires of each individual what their own question is.

The Citizen as Sovereign

As a citizen of Switzerland I feel a confident sense of superiority. This is nothing to be excited about, it's normal. A person who feels politically superior regards politics with less agitation and greater objectivity. The way they see politicians is more like the way one sees employees than the way one sees one's boss. By dint of my right to popular initiative, I can set new impulses in the workings of politics, and with optional and mandatory referendum I have the power to rein the politicians back. The very existence of these possibilities is a quite effective measure against arrogant behavior. This makes the politician more like a blue-collar worker than a building contractor. Politicians here are connected more with the task at hand and less with power. In return, they receive more respect and less derision from the people and the press than their colleagues in other representative democracies. Power is more broadly distributed, thus making politics more task-oriented and objective.

In Switzerland, federal politics do not carry as much weight as in most representative democracies. There's no such thing as them up there and me down here, a fragment of the voting population permitted to cast its vote for one of a few different-yet-identical parties. I take part in shaping the nation. This possibility spurs me on and shapes my attitude toward life. The luxury of saying "No, I can't" is no longer an option. Direct democracy calls upon my will. My voice counts and carries weight: "Yes, I can."

In a direct democracy I feel confident and in charge, because I have the final say. And since I have it, I am seldom forced to make use of it. For the politicians, I am the one who makes the wind blow. That's why politicians need to be good at surfing and sailing. In representative democracies, the politicians often seem to have lowered their sails and travel by motorboat, some even by submarine. How can they tell which way the wind is blowing?

Swiss economist Bruno S. Frey researched the possibilities for political participation in Swiss cantons and found out that people are happier in places where political participation is higher and hurdles to the popular initiatives are lower. According to Frey, by and large "the economic level of a country is higher, the better developed the possibilities are for the population to make its voice heard by means of initiatives and referenda."[59]

In addition, Frey's analyses show, "that democracies with direct participation in political decisions demonstrate considerable economic advantages over other representative democracies. The tax burden is lighter and the government is more efficient, i.e. public services are performed at less cost and with less effort. This is a benefit for economic activity, as there is less bureaucracy and regimentation to deal with."

Direct democracy is an organ of perception. It does not separate; it connects. It teaches me how and why the others think the way they do. Thus for the Swiss, the constitutional referendum is an educational event, one that makes us more mobile, more prudent and sensible.

Unconditional basic income is the next step for democracy. It paves the way to a society where everyone can decide for themselves what they want to do. That benefits society, because the individual can concentrate on themselves, hence also on the question of what they want to bring about in life and where they want to show commitment. Swiss politician and political scientist Andreas Gross sums it up: "The implementation of basic income would be an essential contribution to the democratization of democracy."[60]

Not More, just Better Regulation

Unconditional basic income sees to it that a lot of things currently regulated by the state can be left to its citizens to decide for themselves. If the citizens are provided for at the basic level, there is less need for additional measures and the concomitant imposition of restrictions.

With basic income, instead of having to cut working hours it will be possible for the individual to work according both to demand and to their own needs. With basic income work is no longer something a person has to do, but rather wants to do. Work is the contribution I want to make, not the obligation I have to meet in order to survive.

Basic income doesn't call for a minimum wage. A minimum wage is only necessary as long as there is no basic income. A minimum wage is needed where people are dependent on work and for this reason must demand a minimum price for the work they do. Setting a minimum wage is a right step, but in the wrong direction. It guarantees suitable remuneration for gainful employment. However, it limits paid employment at the same time by making it more expensive. The more expensive work is, the more liable it is to becoming rationalized. The more poorly paid a job is, the more liable it is to not becoming rationalized. Out of fear that jobs would be eliminated, the 2014 Swiss initiative for a minimum wage received the support of only 23% of citizens eligible to vote, and was rejected by every canton.[61]

And in 2013 the maximum wage called for by the 1:12 initiative received just 35% approval and was rejected without receiving approval from a single canton.[62] In the course of the national debate, the worst-case scenario was sketched in which many jobs would be lost, this time on account of income capping. Basic income would address the problem of this kind of rip-off differently: It would create the freedom to turn one's back on companies whose CEOs are too highly paid. It would alleviate the necessity for tedious political battles, because it would put every single person in a position to decide where to commit themselves. If you want to win someone for your cause, you have to demonstrate that your cause is worthwhile. If you succeed at this, other people will commit to the cause. If you only want to take advantage of someone for the sake of a cause the person does not think is meaningful, you leave the arena as a loser.

Before the constitutional referendum on both the minimum wage initiative and the maximum wage initiative, warnings of job losses were issued. Basic income causes the elimination of work that is not meaningful, but it ensures income for work that is meaningful. This makes the individual less susceptible to manipulation, and as a result fewer restrictive or coercing rules are required since each person can settle their own affairs independently.

Switzerland, Germany, the USA

The debate on unconditional basic income varies from country to country. In Switzerland, basic income does not encounter any kind of material need. Here, it is not a solution to any kind of problem. It is not the weapon long yearned for in the war on poverty. It is not the urgently needed instrument for bolstering the economy. In Switzerland, basic income is no emergency measure; it is much rather an innovation. Hence it is an improvement that is controversial and by no means desired by everyone. Basic income is a topic of debate because Switzerland can afford it, if it wants to.

That being said, the subject of basic income is a hot potato for Switzerland. This is because it is an insult to everyone for whom human dignity and worth consist in everyone having to fend for oneself. To these people, basic income is an egregiously wrong and dangerous aberration that promises heaven on earth rather than calling on us to come to terms with the less-than-perfect circumstances on earth. Whoever thinks along these lines sees the social contract jeopardized which stipulates helping only those unable to help themselves. Whoever thinks along these lines still sees an economy threatened that barely functions anyway, thanks only to the incentive of paid work; an economy that with the omission of this imperative loses its basis, since without it everyone can do whatever they want instead of being assigned by the invisible hand of the market what the economy needs. And besides, to many a liberal soul basic income seems like a socialistic specter, a fatal state pension intended to fetter the unfolding of the individual. Those on the left, for their part, fear for the dismantlement of the social benefits they have fought so hard to attain. They depict basic income as neoliberal stripping back, and demand that their embattled social benefits be further expanded instead.

We find this morally charged debate, which feeds on people's hopes and fears, in a radicalized form in Germany as well, which about ten years ago forged an unholy alliance of social and penal legislation that is a slap in the face of its own constitutional law. The consequences of the so-called Hartz-IV benefits victimize not only its recipients, but also those threatened by it in the future, and those whose task it is to administer it on a day-to-day basis. By contrast, these laws are welcomed by all those who decry Germany as a paradise for parasites and slackers, since in their mind's eye they are an effective means of dealing with the plundering of the welfare state.

This situation blocks the German debate on basic income before it can even get underway, owing mainly to the two prejudices that 1) no one would go to work anymore, and 2) there's no way to finance it anyway. The eye of this needle has to be passed through by anyone seeking to get in on the dialog over what basic income could actually do—as a fundamental right longed for by many, because it steps up against a felt sense of forced labor.

In the USA social neediness is far more acute than in Germany; yet there, basic income is sensed less as an emergency measure, than as an innovation, like in Switzerland. The US media response to the Swiss popular initiative bears witness to this. No one seems to place in question the quest by every American to fulfill their American Dream. Under this circumstance any suspicion that nobody would go to work anymore is a moot point. Of course people will go on working—they will simply do what they've always wanted to. They will live their dream.

In the USA, basic income is considered a liberal cause with a liberal tradition. "Feeding programs feed bureaucracy," so the saying goes. Basic income dismantles bureaucracy—i.e. unnecessary mistrust and redundant procedures—by enabling a slimmed-down and more highly effective government, the effect being that it frees its citizens. And anyway: To ever-increasing numbers of young IT enterprisers in Silicon Valley there seems to be no way around furnishing consumers with a basic income. How else are they supposed to be able to afford all the products developed in Silicon Valley for no other purpose than replacing jobs?

So while Switzerland is the place where the most earnest debate on basic income in the world is taking place, Germany lacks the instrument to implement it: a constitutional referendum. Furthermore, the specter of Hartz-IV continues to haunt the land and slight the dignity of all who depend on it in order to survive. In the USA basic income is seen as a liberal promise to enable everyone to do what they want. At the same time, basic income is being discussed in the USA as a means of combatting poverty, because unlike in Germany, where lack is an artificially generated, ethically intended and maliciously organized institution, the USA lacks adequate social benefits to this day. In the USA lack is either not at all perceived as such or sensed as self-evident, for which reason pragmatic measures are being sought to alleviate it. Whereas in Germany it could be eliminated without a problem—if every effort were not being made to maintain it.

Basic Income for Politicians

Why do politicians of all people want to withhold the free space for citizens to make decisions of their own? Politicians already receive a basic income of sorts. They receive an income so they can meet their mandate adequately and not be corrupted. They are not remunerated for the performance of a prescribed task, but for making decisions of their own. So why is it that precisely politicians find it particularly difficult to approve of the idea of an unconditional basic income?

The free mandate is a pillar of representative democracy. Every representative can vote on any ballot as they see fit. Nobody can tell them what to do. No one will dock their pay for voting wrong. The representative of the people is not paid for what they do, but rather for being able to do something. This action can consist in doing or refraining from something, in voting "yes" or voting "no." One way or the other, it is a precious good that the elected representative is not paid for their actions, but rather commissioned to perform them. How to rank them is the decision the voters make on election day. It's not about the money.

No one knows better than politicians what basic income feels like: It feels exactly like the income they draw. But unconditional basic income is for non-politicians as well. It's for each and every citizen. For the craftsman and the engineer, the single mother and the unemployed father, for the perpetual student and the early-retiree, the homeless person and the CEO. Why is it so hard for politicians to support unconditional basic income? Do they think they're better than the rest of us? Don't they trust other citizens to carry out a biographical mandate of their own? Or do they consider obsolete the model by which they themselves are remunerated? Would they prefer being paid by their performance and hence only receiving money when they have demonstrated success in behaving according to what they've been asked to do?

The reasons not to favor basic income are manifold. One of them sticks out especially: the voters. It is not a politician's duty to be the nation's intellectual vanguard. Politicians are not voted into office because they are visionaries, but because they want what the majority thinks is right. The politicians, who sail with the wind of the electorate behind them, will alter their course the very moment this wind changes. They will observe exactly when the electorate entrusts the voters, and not just the politicians, with an unconditional basic income. As long as the politicians have not observed this moment, they will do all they can to preserve the collective from an especially absurd idea.

In a democracy, the apparatus of state is not an organ of initiative; rather, this apparatus sees to the proper functioning of what the electorate wants. Politicians are the last ones to want anything. We always think it's the other way around. However, there will never be a consistently successful politician who champions topics in which no one is interested. The inverse holds as well: There are legions of successful politicians who champion topics that at the moment are particularly hot.

We needn't worry about the politicians. They will do what we want because they want to get elected. Until we want something different, about all they will be good for is serving as a mirror that shows us all the things that haven't yet become self-evident. This indolence is an expression of the democratic path an idea has to travel in order not to become an ideology. Any idea we see all of a sudden being ridden around in droves is a suspect for ideology. This is why unconditional basic income will only come once it has travelled this path so far that the social need for its implementation has long since become obvious to all. When this point has been reached, the parties and politicians who now declare it devious will play their game differently: They will advocate basic income, and they will plead the case for the one or the other particular model according to their respective standpoints. Once it has become clear that people want it, the political battle will continue as to how to implement it. Unfathomable though this might be at times, it's just fine the way it is.

One for All, All for One

The creed goes like this: "One for all, all for one." This is the motto under which the Three Musketeers fight in Alexander Dumas's 1844 novel of the same title. This slogan has a penchant for being the unofficial motto of the Swiss Confederation. It is an expression of independent individuality, of the kind of camaraderie that leaves a person entirely free. Only whoever is free is capable of placing themselves fully at the service of the whole. Only the community that leaves its members free enables commitment on their part. Swiss philosopher Stefan Brotbeck, frames this in the following words: "Only I can liberate myself (no one can relieve me of the task of my liberation). But I cannot do it by myself. The drama of self-liberation is a social one."[63]

"One for all": This can also be an expression of overwrought heroism, of self-righteousness, of hubris. The person who takes themselves too seriously—in relation to others. Or it can be an expression of inappropriate selflessness—the individual who does not take themselves seriously enough. In times of the division of labor and external supply it is the formulation of a fact: I am active for everyone else. The work I do takes care not of me, but of others. That works out best of all when it is done voluntarily and autonomously.

"All for one": This can be an indication of false community spirit. The society that takes itself too seriously over against its individual members. Or it can be an expression of a collective that forgets itself in its actions—because it is focused on a single idol. Its *de facto* meaning today is that each individual wants to be taken care of by the others. No one acts as a self-supplier anymore. Everyone is carried by the accomplishments of the community. The community liberates the single person as a human being, since it liberates them from nature, which previously they had to tend. In former times, individuality consisted in the ability to survive on one's own within nature—today it consists in being safely embedded by and within a community, so as to become an independent individual. Modern individuality no longer consists in the individual neediness that each person solves for themself, but rather in the individual deed that each person carries out for the others.

"One for all, all for one." Expressed in terms of social structure this means: everyone for everyone. This is the fabric of modern living circumstances. Unconditional basic income leads to my being freed by others for the sake of others. This is the foundation of the Musketeers' camaraderie. The Musketeers become capable of action through a commitment in freedom. Basic income enables the individual to serve the collective in the best way possible, and out of this there arises the community's highest goal: To set the individual at liberty to do just that. That is modern Latin: *Unus pro omnibus, omnes pro uno.*

The Conditions of the Unconditional

Obviously, there are conditions attached to being unconditional. Unconditional basic income does not suspend the law and order it is founded on. The unconditional nature it postulates sets it apart from the conditions that hold today for the receipt of social benefits.

Laws regulate what pertains to everybody. They have a general validity. With regard to the receipt of basic income, it is up to the lawmakers to decide what amount to set and the form in which it is to be disbursed. How do children figure in? What about retirees? What about refugees?

Generally speaking, basic income will not be attached to the well-known conditions in power to date. To be sure, there's no denying that a person needs to have been born if they are to receive it. Basic income is for humans, not angels. And once someone has been born? That's basic income for the parents. It's no allowance for the child. And it won't be needed for children in the same amount as for adults. So parents can draw a child's basic income until the child turns adult and as an adult receives a basic income of their own. At all events, basic income will replace child benefits in their full amount. And it will replace all other social benefits in their respective full amounts. Of course everyone reliant on additional financial support would continue receiving it, based on need.

Who should not receive basic income? Stupid people? Lazy people? Sassy, defiant or insolent people? Rich people? Minors? Entrepreneurs? Politicians? Aliens? Is there any reason at all not to receive basic income? Because a person doesn't work? Because a person doesn't want it? Because then other people will get it as well? Because I'm unwilling to accept a basic income from strangers? Because I prefer to fend for myself? Because I don't want others to want it?

The particular conditions of unconditional basic income could be negotiated once everyone has agreed on its implementation. An income that represents an individual legal entitlement to the guarantee of a person's existence and is granted with neither any requirement for service in return nor any eligibility test.

We Are (Not) Family

The family is the welfare state of self-sufficiency, the place where everyone holds their own agricultural court and brings its surpluses to market. It is the place where production and consumption take place according to family law. Marriage is the founding institution of the family, and guarantees the preservation of this community of purpose. It is through this community of purpose that its individual members can bear up under the vicissitudes of life.

What once was a community of purpose has meanwhile become today's needs-based community. In our work-centered society as well, where whoever receives a wage in return for gainful employment is under obligation to take care of the non-gainfully employed portion of their family, this family is still considered the social context that obliges its members to reciprocal solidarity— before one is permitted to turn to the community, the state or the federal government.

It is absurd that today, in times of globalization and individualization, the family should still have to fill the same economic function it was charged with back then. One can go so far as to say that legal obligation on the family's part to function as a solidary collective is actually harmful to the progress of its contemporary development.

Neither individualism nor globalization can qualify the family as a meaningful solidary collective in our times. The former judges a person precisely not based on family ties, while the latter is no more and no less than an expression of worldwide business facilitation.

In terms of services rendered, the individual no longer has any connection with their family and is much rather linked with all human beings the world over. And as an individual, the human being stands in the world at large, and no longer simply as someone else's child, a qualification that for centuries covered the whole territory that defined what an individual was.[64]

While today's protagonist is the free individual, in economic terms we see mankind as a whole, whereas in political terms it is still the national state that matters. The latter embarked on its career as a welfare state at the end of the 19th century under Germany's first imperial chancellor Otto von Bismarck, who was the first head of state to come to the aid of workers unable to generate a livelihood for their families.

While under Bismarck situations of vital urgency were the prerequisite for allotment of family support, today it ought to come with absolutely no strings attached. Isn't it outmoded that parents today are still under obligation to provide for their children—and later children for their parents? These obligations, far from de-economizing the family, continue to exploit it financially, which leads in turn to financial inbreeding that impedes the free unfolding of all involved.

German Journalist Arno Widmann writes in the *Berliner Zeitung*: "If the family has become nothing more than a segment in a person's life, lawmakers are under obligation to redefine the allocation of responsibilities that exist between the individual, the family, society and the government. The greater the individualization that a society undergoes, the smaller the role becomes that mediating institutions play, and the more—there is no pleasure in stating this, but it is the bitter truth—immediate the connection becomes between the citizen and the government. This makes the call for a basic income for every citizen all the more urgent."[65]

Whether or not the taste of this truth is bitter need not concern us here; whatever the case may be, basic income is an opportunity to support the individual and to relieve the family of this burden. That means a lot. After all, the many demographic issues ranging from the birth rate to care for the aging can only be resolved at the family level if and when the family has ceased being an economic collective; that is, once it is no longer made to function as the distorted picture of a once-legitimate social collective whose distinguishing feature was that each of its members—and hence also each family unit—were able to provide for itself.

A state consisting of individuals in an economy based on external supply is not made up of families, but of citizens. Nowadays, the head of a household does not cast his single vote on behalf of every member of the household; each individual person votes for themselves. The individual is the unit of measurement for all matters. Basic income is an investment in the process of individualization. It supplies the start-up capital for the biographical venture that each individual undertakes.

Emancipation for Everyone

Emancipation means liberation from paternal custody. Today's social state is still established on the principle that those unable to take care of themselves be provided for, as long as they can demonstrate their own neediness. Unconditional basic income breaks with this. Neediness no longer need be demonstrated. For a good reason: Whoever declares their neediness to someone cannot avoid putting themselves under the control of that person. The person in need becomes a supplicant. This is not a position of sovereignty. It is begging in its modern form.

Why do beggars sit on the ground? Because it is not possible to beg from the charitable person on the same level. The gesture one makes to demonstrate one's neediness would not be sincere any other way. Anyone who approaches a person on the same level is not begging, but negotiating. The beggar lives from their lack of being on the same level—just as the donor does. That is why basic income is unattractive to those who like being charitable and granting things to others. Basic income ends the culture of alms. Alms are based on pity. And one cannot pity someone who is doing well.

Let's not underestimate the social relevance of the constellation where some are donors and others are receivers. People who give have power. People who receive feel obligated. Basic income puts an end to this. I don't have to be grateful and subservient any longer. I take control. I do not receive basic income because I need it, but because I am a human being. I am the reason for basic income, not my neediness. We give each other mutual permission to live. Unconditionally. This is the highest form of emancipation. Not: Those people up there give to those people down there. Instead: Everyone receives from everyone else. Basic income tares the scales.

One might think that everyone would then become dependent on the government. What would actually happen, though, is that unconditional basic income would emancipate us from government aid. The government could give up treating its citizens like children. The domineering and controlling duties of the state could finally diminish. Basic income commissions the state not to prescribe its people's existence (liberal), but to guarantee it (social). Basic income empowers us to emancipate ourselves from domination by the government and to meet each other in a new way as equals.

Working Capacity as Welfare Benefit

Subsidiarity is a principle of freedom. The pharaoh, who told his people what to do based on divine authority, would not have been fond of this principle. On the contrary: The rulership pyramid at whose peak stands the one and at whose base stand the many, is founded on the many doing as the one says. Their responsibility is not their own; rather, their responsibility to follow his commands. The individual does not yet exist as an entity in their own right. They have not yet acquired a right to problems of their own or to resolve them.

It is not until a state, as a legal entity, renounces any and all absolutism that it grants the individual the free space to determine themselves. This being the case, it is an achievement of the Age of Enlightenment, that aid cannot be dictated from on high for no reason; rather, the individual must wish it and the collective accept it for it to be paid. Only when aid is justified is it a real help and not heteronomy. Only when aid is authorized is it a real help and not a social fraud. It is everyone's right and duty to solve their own problems—and when a person is unsuccessful at it or when it is not just a matter of this person's own problems but of other people's as well, the next-higher level of government takes them up. In this way, the principle of subsidiarity is a prerequisite of all federal governments and their alliances, as well as a central element of free-market economy.

For anyone who construes unconditional basic income the ancient Egyptian way, it seems to have a fatal effect. Just like in the time of the pharaohs, everything good comes from on high rather than from below; from the paternal state rather than from mature citizens, from something abstract and absolute rather than from concrete individuals. Instead of the individual determining themselves in addition to their family, village, region, country and continent, they are made to rely on forced monetary payouts. This amounts not only to patronization, but to waste as well.

But even the subsidiarity of self-help presupposes political and economic circumstances that, to be sure, were not yet in place during the age of the pharaohs, but which were nevertheless valid only until the Age of Enlightenment. Circumstances of this kind are long since outdated. Economy today is world economy. Politics today are world politics. We live in different places, but we live in constant economic and political interdependency. We do our voting and our shopping in a global village. The climate does not care about subsidiarity or the division of labor. The individual and the global community are, meanwhile, on the same level. How can individual freedom and the demands of the collective be connected?

The great challenge we face today is the freedom of others. I help to carry the responsibility for other people's freedom. Inasmuch as I take hold of this responsibility properly, I set others free. I take care of them, so that they can take care of me. This thought inverts the classic principle of subsidiarity: It is no longer a matter of helping others help themselves, no longer a matter of how best to perform my work; rather, it is a question of helping others to help others; of how I can help others help me. I am active no longer for myself, but for others, and they are active for me. Those are the *de facto* social benefits we provide for each other.

Unconditional basic income is not social benefits. It enables social benefit. Social benefit means being active for others—which we always are in a society based on division of labor. Basic income makes this transparent. As it does so, it overcomes a notion of subsidiarity stemming from an era when the individual was awakening to themselves, but also still tilled their own field. This was their self-responsibility. Today, self-responsibility is always respon-sibility for others. With a basic income I can assume this responsi-bility to the best of my belief. The other person can only become an issue for me if my own existence is guaranteed with no ques-tions asked. If everyone receives an unconditional basic income, subsidiarity attains its actual goal: the individual that holds the modern world together.

What Is Fair?

Justice is a question of viewpoint. A cake can be passed out accord-ing to different points of view: numeric fairness (everyone gets a piece of the same size), need-based fairness (everyone gets as much as they need to satisfy their appetite), fairness according to work performance (everyone gets as much as they contributed to mak-ing the cake), ecological fairness (everyone gets as little as possible, so that the cake lasts as long as possible), fairness to oneself (every-one takes as much away from the others as he can).

Fairness means weighing the different points of view as ra-tionally as possible and striving to do justice both to the situation and to the individuals. This is the balancing act which is justice. German philosopher of law Gustav Radbruch writes: "Justice contains an insurmountable tension: Equality is its essence, thus commonality is its form—accordingly, there is a striving inherent in it to do justice both to the uniqueness of the individual occur-rence and to the individual human being."[66]

Unconditional basic income is fair, because it is equal for eve-ryone and at the same time makes it possible for each individual to be different. Basic income creates an equal starting position for all, so that each person can undergo an entirely individual develop-ment. The possibility to make free decisions promotes justice.

One might object that it is unjust to receive money without having worked to earn it. This argument is invalid, though. Justice means not having to work first in order to have an income. Payment of wages only for work done in advance is a gesture of latent mistrust. It is unfair to assume that a person is basically unwilling to work. Justice means no one can condemn us to do something we do not want to do.

Once again: It simply has to be unfair for someone who has not performed any kind of service to receive an income, doesn't it? No. It is unfair when services we render without pay go unseen. It is unfair to act as if gainful employment were the only kind of work there is.

Yes, but isn't it really unfair for the wealthy to receive an unconditional basic income? No, if they didn't receive one, that would be unfair. It would be unfair to exclude them as the upper class. This exclusion of the wealthy would be even more unfair toward people without much money, since the only reason for allowing them a basic income would be that they are short on money. This would be branding them right away as not equal. That is unfair, because every human being is a human being and unconditional basic income is intended not for poor people or for rich people, for smart people or for stupid people, but for human beings.

Who little Risks becomes Reckless

What's the worst thing that could happen if unconditional basic income was introduced? The best thing! That is, the truth would come to light. It might just be that the other people think in an entirely different way about the future than I do—and that now they all suddenly want to take a different track. That would be painful. But above all it would be good if such a difference were made clear once and for all.

With basic income, nothing terrible will happen; all that will happen is what we want to happen. Terrible is what happens as long as there is no basic income. As long as there is no basic income, the biggest insurance company in the world answers to the name "excuse." This name gets all the blame for what we didn't want but ended up doing anyway, or for what we wanted—apparently—but ended up not doing. Unconditional basic income sets up the big closeout on excuses.

There is great fear as to what might happen if unconditional basic income were to be introduced: The great social contract would be severed, the economy would break down, nobody would go to work anymore, we would be endangering our high standard of living, nobody would seek professional training anymore, everyone would retire and stay at home. Yes, this is what we think of one another.

There is no way we can insure ourselves against the truth. The truth can only make us sure of ourselves. There's no getting around taking this risk—unless we would rather make shoddy arrangements with lies. If everyone—myself excepted, of course—really would prefer to return to the stone age, basic income would bring it into the light. And that would be a good thing. After all, why should we call something wealth that no one truly considers to be wealth? In other words, the fewer people there are who actually live the way they want to, the greater the long-term risk of living together will become. Living together is all the more reckless, the more people there are who do not live the way they really want to. Anyone who doesn't live the way they want to turns into a ticking time bomb.

However, with basic income, everything just could turn out quite differently. That is, almost everything might stay the way it is. Except now we would be freer and more autonomous. It might just turn out that, after all, nearly everyone appreciates the division of labor and external supply, fairness and taking initiative. And that with basic income they themselves are finally no longer underappreciated.

In conversations—one-on-one conversations—one has, there are hints as to whether basic income will bring a rude awakening or a pleasant one. The fewest of us wish a return to the Middle Ages. And most of us wish to overcome the structural Middle Ages we are caught in to this day—even if it involves no more than getting past our delusions of self-sufficiency.

In the Middle Ages human destiny approached humanity from the outside, as fate. The human race was impotent in terms of its fate. Such submissiveness to fate was at the same time the foundation of human dignity. The dignity of the modern age lies in power over one's destiny. Today, it is in taking hold of our own destiny that we find our dignity.

Who will Come when Basic Income Comes?

Reasons for abandoning one's homeland are diverse. Some flee starvation and war, others bad weather and uncivil neighbors. One way or the other, on arriving in a new place, someone is what they were when they left their old place: a stranger.

Being foreign or native disappears in a globalized world. This phenomenon is emerging more and more. Not only products circulate the globe; people do as well. These days everyone know a commuter who drives a great distance to work and back every day, a colleague who owns a second apartment near company headquarters, or a businessman who feels more at home in a jet than anywhere else.

There are as many reasons for looking for a new home as there are for leaving the old one. Sometimes it's to seek peace and safety, sometimes to find wealth and self-realization, sometimes it's the scenery, sometimes cultural preferences.

The refugee dramas we are currently witness to in Europe are traumatic. A lot of people who travel arduous routes seeking access to the fortress which is Europe do not do so because they want to encounter low temperatures and unfriendly people—or even because they have had enough of their own culture. They do so for the simple reason that where they come from they lack a basis to live on. This is migration not for the purpose of self-realization, but for the purpose of establishing conditions under which to survive.

Every human being's survival is worth guaranteeing. This is why there is no better developmental policy than unconditional basic income. The main thing a lot of people lack in order to become active is an income. There's enough to do, no matter where. Anyone who thinks there is not enough work is either blind or a cynic.

If we are indifferent to other people's welfare, both they and we will be the worse off for it. It is an illusion to believe that any sort of walls or fences could sever the worldwide cohesion of humanity. We are connected with each other, and the more we tend to and care for this connection, the less people will migrate for the sake of securing their existence.

There is no substance to the fear that basic income would cause an increase in migration. Basic income has a neutral influence on migration. Migration is regulated by emigration law. Basic income will neither make it more acute nor cause it to diminish. Social benefits already are an incentive for coming to Europe. But this is not the true issue. The chief motive for migration is the threat to a person's existence in their homeland.

It is indeed conceivable that unconditional basic income might develop a kind of suction—as a hot export article, that is. Sooner or later, no country with any interest in a functional society and any desire to halt the exodus of its inhabitants will be able to get around basic income. No one who has found their task in life asks if it is better paid somewhere else; this person is simply happy that they can take up this task. Unconditional basic income makes it possible to do what needs to be done and in those places where it is needed most. And it enables us to help others who are less successful at it.

It is an absurd notion not to want something because it might also be of benefit for others. Not doing a good thing because it helps others as well is absolutely bad. If a society were to strive not to improve for the sole reason of preventing others from improving, mankind would not invent or innovate anything. Denying progress in order to prevent others' progress is backward in the extreme.

A good idea develops a dynamic of its own: First everyone wants to get in on it, then they all want to improve on it. So it is quite conceivable that at the beginning the whole world might indeed want to draw a basic income in Switzerland. That is impossible, of course. And so it's quite conceivable that basic income might come to be introduced everywhere in countries that are not Switzerland. It is quite conceivable that the next Swiss export product will not be cheese or chocolate, but an idea: unconditional basic income. The time for unconditional basic income has come. Why shouldn't Switzerland be the first place whose time has come?

Basic Income as Property

To many, basic income seems like a very nice idea that is nevertheless completely off the wall: Everyone is supposed to receive an income entirely irrespective of their salary, to which they are entitled simply because they are citizens. Just like that. Because they are citizens. With no strings attached. There's no way to finance it, say some. It's unfair, say others. It lowers a person's motivation to work, say some. It subsidizes wages, say others. It's capitalism, scold some. It's socialism, fear others.

Why did the idea ever come up in the first place? The welfare state invented by Bismarck can function in the long run only if traditional family forms predominate, and if a low life expectation and uninterrupted employment status are the rule. If they become the exception, if people change jobs, their life-partner and their domicile often, if phases of rest and phases of activity alternate frequently, if ever more machines create material wealth, what needs to be done is not to secure employment, but to make it possible. Then it's not a matter of distributing alms, but of opening up chances. This is what an unconditional basic income does.

As early as the 16th century, Thomas More called not for the death penalty, but for guaranteed income as a means of fighting crime. Thomas Paine wanted in the 18th century to compensate every citizens' God-given right to a piece of land by means of a lump-sum payment. And in the 19th century John Stuart Mill wanted to grant each citizen a basic provision in order to better enable them to make their capacities available.

If we understand basic income not as a welfare payment, but rather as a fundamental right, Thomas Paine's thoughts as articulated in his pamphlet on *Agrarian Justice* (1797) are particularly revealing: Not everyone can be provided with a piece of land when they are born, because private ownership has made this impossible. And so basic income must compensate for this loss "every person, rich or poor," because "it is in lieu of the natural inheritance, which, as a right, belongs to every man, over and above the property he may have created or inherited from those who did."[67]

What was valid in Paine's time is now more valid than ever: A parcel of land doesn't help anyone along, as we have long since left agrarian self-sufficiency behind us. Seen in this way, basic income is a fundamental property for the purpose of undertaking one's life in the 21st century.

Basic income is no socialist real experiment and no neoliberal purgatory on earth. It is rather a third path: It is more socialistic than any socialism, because it guarantees everyone a minimum amount regardless of what they accomplish and without stipulating any kind of work, but without giving up the added value of the free-market economy along with the forces of innovation and rationalization inherent in it. This makes basic income at the same time more capitalistic than any capitalism, because it supplies everyone with a consumer's allowance, through which the free-market economy can first get underway, because everyone's existence is guaranteed as a fundamental right.

Unconditional basic income calls for a system change in our heads. It breaks with the past rhetoric of give and take, of guaranteeing jobs, of incentives for the unemployed. It wants the whole human being, but it doesn't want to take this human being anywhere. It grants each person their own individual planned economy and leaves the free-market economy up to us all. It leaves us free and ensures us—and these are the noblest tasks there are in the present day.

And Who is Going to Pay for it All?

Who's supposed to pay for basic income? This is the best of all the false questions. Basic income doesn't need to be paid for; it needs to be understood. In monetary terms it is a zero-sum game. It is not an additional income; it is a fundamental one. It does not lead to more money in the bank, but to the same funds being composed in a different way. As a rule, the other income earned previously drop in the amount of basic income a person draws. The account balance stays the same.

Unconditional basic income constitutes the pedestal of our total income. This unconditionality requires not money, but trust. Once I have understood this, I don't have a question concerning payment, but storytelling. I do have a question concerning how to come up with what an unconditional basic income is capable of doing for myself, for my neighbors, at school, at work, in politics.

We know what conditional income is. Today all of us have a more or less conditional income at our disposal, in the form of money earned from working or from capital gains, either private or government transfer payments. It is not possible to live today with no income. Government benefits stem from taxes and social insurance contributions. People receive them based on old age, unemployment or illness. Unconditional basic income is not income received by only those people who need it. It is not a social benefit, not a form of charity, not a wage. It is not a purchase, it is not a form of barter, nor is it a gift. It is founded on the insight that today everyone who lives needs an income to do so. It asks if it wouldn't be more reasonable to detach the guarantee for a person's existence from all and sundry conditions.

If we want to guarantee people's existence unconditionally, the question arises as to how we are to disburse basic income. This question is not the topic of the Swiss popular initiative. All the same: Even now there are different modes of disbursement currently under discussion, and different types of taxes that are being compared with each other. Some count on wealth tax, others find an added value tax suitable, yet others want basic income to be financed by means of a tax on financial transactions. What all these possibilities have in common is that they favor suggestions for financing which lead beyond unconditional basic income. If we want unconditional basic income, the next big topic will be how we intend to deliver it.[68]

It is no wonder that countless numbers are in circulation concerning basic income. Attempts are made to confirm or to disprove different financing models. There is nothing wrong with that, but it does tend to be a source of confusion more than a help. This is because anyone who seeks to prove their own model does so by making use of assumptions that cause everything to appear completely logical and obvious, or fully absurd and unrealistic.

The question of how to finance basic income is also employed as a means of disguising one's own subjective ill will as something objective. People who don't want basic income prefer to say that it cannot be financed, rather than that they don't trust their fellow citizens. Being at the mercy of a pseudo-question that does not ask what it purports to ask is not a matter that involves basic income alone: In times that prefer numbers over words, the financing question has become the preferred tactic of distracting others from noticing that one simply doesn't want it. Not infrequently do people who claims that something cannot be financed do so in full knowledge that they are using a cliché intended to render any further discussion on the topic superfluous. In so doing, these people ignore this essential insight by German theologian Oswald von Nell-Breuning: "Anything capable of being generated in a free-market economy [...] is in turn capable of being financed. The only precondition is that people honestly and seriously want it."[69]

The actual question regarding basic income is the question pertaining to the consequences of it being unconditional: What consequences would unconditional basic income have on the development of the economy and of society? Would it cause paralysis or dynamic mobility? Would it have a hampering or a promoting effect? Would we become active in a motivated and perceptive way for work that needs to be done? Or would we cease working and no longer get involved? These are research questions that no financing model can answer. Only we ourselves can do that. German journalist Wolf Lotter draws this resume concerning basic income: "Its ability to be financed is guaranteed. Where we need practice is in exercising freedom."[70]

The Redistribution of Power

Who is actually in possession of power, anyway? Is it the person who does something? Yes, if what they do is free. Anyone who does what they want has power. Anyone forced to do what they do not want is impotent. Power bears witness to skill, capability, capacity. Impotence expresses not being able to do something.

Do the people with money have power? Yes, because they can do what they want and do not have to do what others want them to. Furthermore, whoever has money can determine what other people do. What they do not want to do they can have other people do for money. Unless the other people also have money. In this case, money loses its power to make people do things. Then it is the person who does something who has power. If everyone has money, no one has to do what they do not want to do.

Not only money endows people with power; so does knowledge. The ignorant are powerless. We also have power in those places where we direct our attention. This is why the media have power. They do not have the power to make us look, but when we do look, it is the media that direct our gaze.

What does unconditional basic income alter in the existing distribution of power? The fear we have for our existence loses its ground. Existential fear makes us impotent. Anyone whose position in life is determined by fear for their existence can be more easily led astray than someone who doesn't have any existential worries. The person whose existence is guaranteed is much freer than the person whose existence is constantly at issue.

Whoever has to do something is not accountable in the same way as those who want to do something. Taking action out of necessity restricts a person's responsibility. We cannot make someone who didn't want to do the thing they did accountable to the same extent as we can someone who did something of their own free will. Freedom of will makes criminal liability possible. Whoever is accessory to upholding the unfree situation carries part of the responsibility for the unfree action.

According to Max Weber, power means being able to assert one's own will against the will of others.[71] That is not power, but violence, says Hannah Arendt.[72] Power and violence are opposites. People who have no power resort to violence. Violence is a demonstration of powerlessness. Violence is heteronomy. Power is autonomy. Power makes for enthusiasm. Power is empowering. Power enables others to participate.

In the future, those will be in possession of power who can do something that machines cannot do. Whoever thinks independently has power. Whoever can make free decisions has power. Whoever does not have to do anything has power. Unconditional basic income empowers people to self-determination. This is a redistribution of power. It now lies entirely in the hands of the individual.

All Those In Favor

Act of Liberation

"The economy has an obligation not just to produce goods, but also to liberate people from work. [...] We live in paradisiacal circumstances. The question is: How can we manage to grant everyone access to what our society produces? [...] We have no need of a right to work. We need a right to an income. To an unconditional basic income [...] The entrepreneurs would lose power, the unions, the politicians also would lose power and influence. But every citizen would win dignity, security and real freedom."[73]

Götz W. Werner, entrepreneur

Defense of Democracy

"In a world where the value of formal work decreases ever more, basic income is one of the most urgent ideas there are. Unemployment will increase and we can no longer be certain that there will always be jobs for everyone. What is certain, though, is that everyone needs to eat. Basic income prevents people from being thrown back into fearing for their existence and into despair. Seen in this way, a regular basic income is also a contribution to the defense of democracy, to our social contract, and ultimately to our civilization at large."[74]

Jean Ziegler, politician

Updated Civil Rights

"Do we want to force everyone to compete with each other in selling themselves? Or would we rather have a radical alternative: a civilized, highly-developed society with up-to-date civil rights—part and parcel of which are socio-economic rights? [...] If everyone receives an unconditional basic income, stigmatization will stop. Having a universal civil right is completely different than belonging to the 'failures' who are dependent on welfare benefits."[75]

Peter Ulrich, economist

Laziness doesn't Pay

"Basic income would not cause society to plunge into a ubiquitous laziness. On the contrary: Thanks to basic income people would no longer have to resort to generating as much money as possible and could afford job training in low-paying businesses. [...] For five years I have been enjoying the freedom to do what I want. [...] This new freedom has been a vital experience for me. I believe that is what the effect of an unconditional basic income would be for everyone. [...] The world would be a better place, a place with fewer jobless people, with more people able to do what they really want to."[76]

Oswald Sigg, politician

Full Employment is Backward

"I see unconditional basic income as a necessary consequence of the economic development our time has undergone. This is because we build machines that eliminate hard, monotonous work for us. There are less and less jobs where people have to slave away. That's a good thing. Under these circumstances, though, I think it is backward to try and uphold the goal of full employment. All it does is make us place more and more people in temporary jobs, in dangerous jobs, in part-time jobs—and in work purely for the sake of being occupied."[77]

Marina Weisband, politician

Simpler through Transparency

"I believe we need to evaluate basic income within the context of our system as it currently exists. This system is as highly complex as it is untenable. The initiative for basic income forces us to ask the right questions, which are the questions about how to make things simpler. [...] The key thing about basic income is its transparency. It is through transparency and simplicity that we are able to implement direct democracy. [...] The issue of incentives is blown entirely out of proportion. It is a cliché we would do better not to heed."[78]

Klaus W. Wellershoff, economist

Slaughtering the Holiest of Cows

"The initiative for basic income slaughters our holiest cow and gets the precept by the throat which states: 'No work, no food.' That's a hard one to top. The initiative asks questions on the sense and nonsense of work, on exploitation and the right to a life. It asks what obligation is and whether or not working at home with children, the elderly, the handicapped, or with flowers ought not to be remunerated. It asks the question concerning overblown welfare systems and capitalism. [...] Switzerland has taken up the debate. Well done!"[79]

Linard Bardill, songwriter

Time for Things that Matter

"Most people—even if they do badly paid work—take joy in contributing to the welfare of everyone. But our work-centered society is strongly orientated towards money. Every single minute has to be accounted for. We see this in the caregiving professions, where time for the patient is no longer provided for. Basic income would enable us to ask question concerning the meaningfulness of our work without having to fear so much for our existence. People could take time for the things that matter in life. It's a long way before we get there. We ought to re-think what work means to us at all."[80]

Judith Giovannelli-Blocher, author

Creating Freedom instead of Jobs

"Once a basic income has been implemented that is distributed to everyone unconditionally, working will no longer be a matter of securing one's existence [...]; it will rather—and much more importantly—be a matter of the meaning of work itself, and along with it of enhancing the quality of life—whether one's own life or the community's. It is no longer social to create jobs, but to create freedom—the freedom to do what I think is necessary and right."[81]

Ralph Boes, activist

Elimination of Compulsory Measures

"I find sanctioning by the unemployment agency wrong and ir-reconcilable with human dignity. The possibility to implement sanctions and the system of repression connected with it is one of the flaws in the current benefits system. This is why I have stood up for its elimination for quite some time. [...] For several years I have been in favor of introducing an unconditional basic income, mainly because, unlike the current system, it would do away with compulsory measures."[82]

Hans-Christian Ströbele, politician

Flat Rate for Democracy

"Three things are crucial for me. For one thing, with a basic income we can eliminate the fear for our material existence. [...]

The second thing is a radically democratic impulse: I see in un-conditional basic income a kind of all-inclusive flat rate for democracy. [...] The third thing is that in unconditional basic income I actually see a social transformation project. It is admittedly no sure-fire way to overcome capitalism. But with basic income it would at least be easier to stand up for freedom as well as a sustainable and social economy."[83]

Katja Kipping, politician

Free-Market Economy for Free Human Beings

"Unconditional basic income provides certainty, allows for participation and enables initiative. In my estimation, it not only preserves individual freedom; it also enables freedom where until now freedom was restricted. Everyone gets a solid economic basis and can design their own life. Unconditional basic income would turn our free-market economy into a social entity. Whoever wants to work a lot, can; anyone who wants to get rich can undertake to do so, without leaving the ground that guarantees the same freedom for each and every one of us."[84]

Susanne Wiest, activist

Cut Down Bureaucracy

"It ought to be simple to convince sincere critics of bureaucracy and government administration of the advantages of unconditional basic income. Basic income would alleviate having to check up on whether people are poor, employable, entitled to their household's standard of living, or abused in their autonomy and dignity. [...] This would enable us on the job market to assert the very quintessence of freedom: our freedom to say 'no'. At the same time, though, there would be no loss whatsoever of material incentives to say 'yes' to the many chances gainful employment has to offer."[85]

Claus Offe, sociologist

Making the Welfare State Social

"A basic income [...] provides on advance financing in a reliable way. It is the guarantee for entrepreneurial, professional, and joint activities. This does not cause the nationalization of society; it only makes the welfare state social. [...] Basic income's guarantee can be integrated into liberal, conservative, socialistic-social democratic conceptions of public order. And so it fits quite well into a globalized world where Bismarck's welfare state appears increasingly anachronistic."[86]

Michael Opielka, sociologist

Further Advances in Rationalization

"Society will not give up technological and social innovation, nor should it. However, industrially developed nations have failed so far at distributing fairly—that is, to everyone's benefit—the advances made through rationalization. The result is left-over activities, de-qualification and unemployment for some, and densely compacted work, self-exploitation and exhaustion for others. [...] Basic income will not make anyone lazy, any more than gainful employment makes anyone intrinsically hardworking. Humans beings are, quite simply, beings of activity."[87]

Theo Wehner, industrial psychologist

Socio-Political Revolution

"The free-market economy banks on individual willingness to take risks. Solidary citizens' income strengthens people's willingness to see risks as chances. Because they cannot fall below the existential minimum, people will be more willing to take risks, to be creative. Motivation occurs not through coercion and control, but through trust and incentive. Citizens' income is not a sofa; it's a diving board. [...] We need the courage to undertake a socio-political revolution."[88]

Dieter Althaus, politician

Prevention instead of Repair

"No social policy claiming to do justice to the realities of life may limit itself to helping people in need. All social policy must likewise prevent people from becoming needy in the first place. That is, prevention, not repair is called for; enabling work rather than guaranteeing it. Enabling people instead of treating them as wards. In short: Opening up chances instead of giving handouts. Basic income is fully aligned with the future. It sees to it that everyone [...] receives a government transfer payment in the amount of the minimum standard of living. This transfer payment comes with no strings attached, no actions required in return, no application procedure and hence no red tape whatsoever. It is distributed as a universal transfer payment."[89]

Thomas Straubhaar, economist

A Chance to Walk Upright

"Maybe we as a labor union need to redefine our goal for full employment. Maybe we need to say that full employment is not everyone engaging in gainful employment, but rather everyone being able to live the way they want to. [...] But unconditional basic income also means that people won't have to drop to their knees whenever they need financial support for a time, [...] it allows them to walk upright and to find their own way into the future."[90]

Kurt Regotz, unionist

Better than Party Politics

"We all know we need to remodel our work-centered society and detach our social security systems from the factor of work. All of us are thinking about basic income and citizens' income, but none of the parties have the courage to propose it. [...] We all know that more and more people are drawing money from the social security system and that less and less people will be paying into them in the future. So there's no getting around rebuilding the system. But no one has actually taken the topic up. Instead, we are performing plastic surgery on a cancer patient."[91]

Richard David Precht, author

Beyond Sanctions and Subsidies

"Neither market radicalism, which considers humans to require work incentives, nor protective public care, which considers subsidies to be the highest goal, is willing to grant citizens the chance to decide for themselves. What today comes along in the form of counseling, but at the same time sanctions people to keep them under pressure, is an expression of helplessness over the failure of all strategies to date. [...] Our collective community can only survive if we as citizens are free to make our own decisions. This is the foundation of our democratic law and order by, of and for the freedom of the individual. Basic income would be no more and no less than the next step in its evolution."[92]

Sascha Liebermann, sociologist

A Question of Dignity

"The welfare state has been turned upside down. It's time to put it back onto its feet. Time for basic income. Enough for each person. And let no one come along with the food-for-work ethic of past epochs. Or with the objection that basic income is unfair toward anyone who works hard to earn their money. Work performance and fairness are now precisely not the crucial principles of our system. No connection exists between virtue and work performance, and in our system fairness is a matter of pure accident. Modern capitalism has long since cast these values overboard. Basic income gives the people back their dignity."[93]

Jakob Augstein, journalist

People aren't Parasites

"If you leave people the decision how they want to contribute to society, they would probably do something more valuable than you would have come up with when you decided to force them to do something. Most people actually don't want to be parasites— maybe a few, but not enough to make a difference. I always like the example of prisons: Even in high security prisons, people are handled fairly well, they get food and shelter, and all their basic needs are taken care of. Their punishment is that they are not allowed to work. Everyone wants to work and make something out of their lives."[94]

David Graeber, anthropologist

Relief for the Government

"I personally am a big fan of universal basic income as a total means of disengaging base income from labor. [...] No one has been able to convince me that there is any other way. [...] If we have a guaranteed basic income, a lot of issues currently handled by the state, like education and housing, can be resolved privately. [...] Basic income would lead to greater flexibility, more commerce and a bigger market than the solutions we currently employ."[95]

Albert Wenger, investor

Humanizing Labor

"Whether the coming economic order is a sharing economy or an on-demand economy it will only function if it is ensured by means of an unconditional basic income. That is, it will only function if every man, woman and child, retirees included, automatically receives an amount that enables them to live a life in dignity. Seen this way, basic income is not a romantic illusion for people out in left field, but much rather the prerequisite for a new world of work, a world in which thanks to robots and artificial intelligence humans can work under more humane conditions; but only if society really guarantees their livelihood."[96]

Philipp Löpfe, journalist

From Person to Person

"The question involved in unconditional basic income is whether I acknowledge people as entities. Everyone. Whether I can sense the essence of their being. If I cannot, it's pretty clear that, ethics, morality and what have you don't have any substance either. That makes them a negotiable mass. And that is how we handle interpersonal encounters today. All unconditional basic income does is make things rather clear. It's not a romantic fantasy. And it doesn't have a particular image of what a human being is. All it has is an general one."[97]

Enno Schmidt, painter

Making a Rounder World

"The flat world needs to be rounded once more. What counts with unconditional basic income is that it makes the world even rounder yet. It's not the answer to all our questions, but it is a technique for concentrating on bigger questions rather than on wrong answers. Such is this initiative's cultural point of departure." [98]

Adolf Muschg, author

How Free Are We if We Stop Coercing Others?

The Compulsion of Freedom

Unconditional basic income is not a path to freedom; it leads rather into bondage. Or so a number of its critics claim. It is excessive socio-political regulation and an excessive demand on human beings generally. At best it frees a minority of the creative class, but otherwise it broadcasts a dire watchword: holidays, not hard work; lethargy, not productivity; making babies, not baking bread.

Notwithstanding the fact that basic income is no welfare benefit, but a fundamental right; does not bloat bureaucracy, but cuts red tape; does not interfere with work, but enables it; does not amount to a tax hike; but to a tax disbursement—notwithstanding all this, the question of compulsion remains open. What is it that forces us to do something?

The kind of freedom we experience as compulsion is the freedom that is just there. It's there and does not go away. At least not without me making up my mind to give it away. Basic income lets me make choices which might have been possible without it, though certainly not in as radical a manner. Thanks to basic income the question of what I want does not lead me into a life of unfreedom; instead, it becomes a cardinal question. The world no longer dictates what I am to do; it rather asks me what I want to do. That is strenuous—and meaningful. Because anyone who forever lives without questions harms themselves and others. People who never make decisions of their own impede their own individuality.

Swiss author Adolf Muschg underscores the historical significance of this situation: "The Western world started out with Socrates's mode of asking questions. [...] Socrates was put to death for his mode of asking questions—by his own society. [...] There is no one who can take this risk off a person's hands. But it is possible to make the risk an easier one to bear. [...] Unconditional basic income makes it easier to be willing to undertake a new age of inquiry. [...] It is an imaginal dowry that allows for new questions."[99]

Basic income makes the compulsion of freedom—that is, the fact that it is simply given—especially evident, because it causes the compulsion of bondage to let up. It is like the pain caused by the dentist's drilling: The main reason why the coercion of bondage is painful is that it pressures me even though the pressure could be avoided. We live in abundance, yet we are forced lack upon ourselves because we lack ideas. The pain of this fact is bitter. It is a kind of pain that never existed in times of lack. Whenever shortage reigns for everyone, it is clear what needs to be done: Everyone pitches in to eliminate it. That's the dignity of being active in this way, and at the same time it is what makes it so obvious.

The compulsion of basic income is the compulsion of freedom. This is the only compulsion worthy of a liberal society. We learn via basic income that it is impossible to sidestep freedom. What we do of our own free will takes on a worth of its own. It adds not false activism to the world, but rather free actions.

Whoever is in favor of basic income modernizes coercion to become the compulsion of freedom. Anyone who is against basic income forces a compulsion on themselves of which the world has striven for millennia to rid itself. Anyone against basic income mistakes the pain of childbirth with the pain of a decaying tooth. Unconditional basic income is the pain of childbirth. It brings people back down to the earth by allowing them to come into their own. Today's system as it has been handed down to us is the decaying tooth. The procedure for a decaying tooth is to extract it.

Trust as the Basic Currency

Calling for a vote of confidence means wanting to know if one can still rely on the most fundamental of presumptions. Trust is one such fundamental presumption; without trust we could not live. It is the basic currency of existence. The small child is an archetype of this trust. The child lives in pure devotion to and utter trust in the world.

The same holds for adults: In almost everything we do we trust in the reliability of other people. From riding the elevator to behavior in traffic to boarding an airliner, we trust others. But we also trust that the price we pay is fair and that the groceries we eat are not polluted.

Withholding one's trust in the world is a process of individuation. If I put trust in myself rather than in the world and my fellow human beings, I am exerting my individuality, my subjectivity, my existence as a single person. On the other hand, it is only in a society that engenders and supports individuation that this process can be maintained. Without the others I cannot become an individual. Thanks to them, I can.

Unconditional basic income does not make trust redundant. It rather realizes that everyone has unconditional needs, and that if these needs are not met unconditionally trust doesn't have a leg to stand on. People whose existence is threatened cannot be trusted. They play their existential needs off against me. People not afraid for their existence are free for matters that presuppose trust. Only once we trust others do they become genuinely responsible and, as a rule, unwilling to disappoint our trust in them.

Unconditional basic income accomplishes two things: It guarantees the individual person's existence—and it makes this person an individual who is capable of trust. It does not create a problem of mistrust, because the moment one's existence is not on the line one can articulate any issues involving it. While today we always avoid saying the truth or withholding our trust, unconditional basic income makes trust freely accessible, because it ensures people's existence.

Safe Uncertainty

Safe is safe. Whoever feels safe need not take precautionary measures. A space beyond safety comes about. Freedom comes about.

Safety can also be a prison. The insurance prison. Every fear we insure ourselves against spawns' new fears. Hence safety can likewise be grounds for bondage. And insecurity grounds for freedom. Not succumbing to an insecurity is a sign of freedom. Not giving in to fear right away is a sign of courage. Certainty concerning an insecurity one can turn the insecurity around, causing certainty and thus liberation. In the best case, feeling secure permits constructive interaction with insecurity. Existential security is a good basis for taking on insecurity in life.

We have fuses in case something happens, not once they have happened. Then it's too late. Fuses are the result of planning ahead. A fuse makes sense not only after it is blown, but beforehand, so that a short circuit doesn't cause any damage.

Insurance is like a fuse. A large group of individuals pays for insurance in case damage is done, but in the hope that none is. As a member of this group, I pay my insurance bill in the hope that any damage that could occur does not harm me, and for the sake of the certainty that any damage that does happen to me can be paid for out of the contributions made by the whole group. The principle of insuring—in which the collective bears any damage done to individuals—is a solidary action. The fact that insurances have also turned into stock speculators is a different matter.

Insurance is a good thing in case of damage or loss. Being alive, however, is not a form of damage or loss. This is why basic income is not insurance. Basic income does not insure; it is a backup, like a fuse. With basic income, no insurance in the style of social benefits is any longer needed to secure one's existence.

Does freedom provide safety? Yes. Freedom gives a person the certainty of not having to do what they do not want to do. Freedom is a fuse for coercion. Freedom provides the certainty that the person will not be cheated. The certainty of no longer having to do anything leads to the freedom to do many things. This is the promise of freedom that basic income holds.

Money as a Liberal Gift Certificate

Money is a gift certificate. But a gift certificate is not money. Money is a gift certificate that can be put toward anything money can buy. The assortment is huge and the decision is with the person who uses money to pay.

A gift certificate is only good for the item designated on it. A gift certificate for coffee is good for coffee, not for beer. The function of the gift certificate is determined not by the person who received it, but by the one who gave it. With money you can pay. Gift certificates can only be redeemed.

You use money to buy gift certificates; instead of giving someone money, you buy the person a gift certificate. In this way you determine what the person does with the gift certificate. The person can do anything they wants with money. With a gift certificate for the cinema they can only go to the movies. They can choose the film they want to watch, but they cannot go to the theater or to a restaurant instead.

If basic income were issued as a gift certificate for a shopping cart full of the items a person supposedly needs, we as the state would boss the person around saying that we know better and that we are the ones who say what the person needs. We would display skepticism and distrust toward the individual. We would act as their guardian. A gift certificate is earmarked money provided by people who want to control the recipient. Money is a liberal gift certificate.

How Free Is the Market if People Are Unfree?

We have long since lived not in a domestic economy, but in a market economy. Each produces for the other's consumption. The market is the place that matches up producers and consumers when they are no longer one and the same person. Division of labor leads to their separation.

"I have never thought, for my part, that man's freedom consists in his being able to do whatever he wills, but that he should not, by any human power, be forced to do what is against his will." This statement is attributed to Jean-Jacques Rousseau, the Enlightenment philosopher and forerunner of the French Revolution.[100] Measured by this declaration, we have no free labor market today. We are forced to participate in the labor market because the income we receive is conditional instead of unconditional. But a market is only free as long as I am not forced either to purchase or to sell anything. The labor market is free if I can accept a job offer, but do not have to. Unconditional basic income would create a free labor market with no obligation to contract. Fully comprehensive freedom of contract would be a tremendous asset that only unconditional basic income can guarantee.

The notion of freedom that shapes today's conception of the free market is a neoliberal one: Freedom consists in not having to show consideration for others. Freedom is equipped with elbows.

May the better contestant win! According to one neoliberal critic, basic income violates this market principle. It is a spoilsport. People's existence would be guaranteed and competition no longer free to run its course. And what would happen to the winners if there were no losers? What would freedom be worth if it could be guaranteed? Freedom means being able to convince others by means of your accomplishments. Today's job market is free, so the argument goes, since you can choose a new boss anytime you like —as long as you are attractive enough.

This line of argument stands in fundamental contradiction to the perspective of unconditional basic income. Freedom does not mean asserting oneself against others. Freedom does not mean that the right of the stronger prevails. On the contrary: Freedom can only unfold within our awareness of our fellow human beings. This is no mere socio-romantic yarn; it is a fact. Korean philosopher Byung-Chul Han accounts for this when he writes: "Freedom is, basically, a word that involves relationship. The only place a person feels truly free is in a successful relationship, in a fulfilling togetherness with others."[101]

Whoever does not count on another person's freedom need not count on their own. Economic competition must be freed from existential pressure; otherwise it can only lead to suffering rather than to true accomplishments. The free market can only be a path to freedom if it's about excellence and not about existence.

Does Consumer Freedom Make Us Free?

Consumer freedom does not mean being able to buy anything I want. Consumer freedom means that there is nothing I am forced to buy and that I can decide for myself what I buy. The prerequisite to this freedom is that I have the funds at my disposal to allow me maximum freedom to consume. If I have little funding, I likely have little choice but to buy cheap products. The price, not the quality decides. I purchase what is cheap and not necessarily good. My purchase depends more on my financial means than on what I need.

Discount! Sale! Special offer! Hardly anyone can resist this kind of boasting, not even if they could easily afford to pay normal prices. It is simply a good feeling to get something for less, even though everyone knows that both the price reduction and all the taxes and other fees are included in the regular prices. We nevertheless have the feeling that we have received priority treatment and been particularly smart. Paying less for something than it actually costs not only gives us wings to purchase, but also arouses a feeling of satisfaction.

A special price is not an increased amount I pay because the seller is special; it is a reward for my being such a special customer. But why, after all? If people have done something for me, then why is the special price I pay them less rather than more? Why do I feel better when I pay less? What would make it possible for me to feel better by paying more? My understanding that my friends are not my enemies. I would have to understand that everything I consume is the accomplishment of others on my behalf. Then I as the consumer would thank the producers by means of a special price, instead of shaming them by means of an ordinary stingy price.

Unconditional basic income could allow us greater control over our consumer decisions. It could make us more resistant to advertising, it could promote a general focus on quality, sustainability and fair trade. It could reveal the social interconnection between producers and consumers and transform us from hounded bargain hunters into circumspect consumers.

Only What is Superfluous is Necessary

The Spanish philosopher José Ortega y Gasset distinguishes between human activities that are necessary and those that are superfluous. In his assessment, everything that is necessary is what humans have to do to see to their livelihood—that is, getting enough to eat, a roof over their heads and clothing on their backs. Everything else is superfluous: literature, music, philosophy, art, science, religion, in a word everything we associate with culture. But here's the remarkable thing about Ortega y Gasset: In his estimation, the only thing the human being really needs is what is objectively superfluous.[102]

What does this mean? It is true that even in the natural world not everything is determined by necessity. If it were, the birds would sing less and it would be quieter on pleasant summer evenings. Thus all it takes to refute Darwin's theory of the survival of the fittest is the birds' singing. But, as Ortega y Gasset says, the only creature who indulges in superfluity wholeheartedly and with complete fervor is the human being. Throughout history humanity has even been willing to accept restrictions in the necessities of life for the sake of indulging the superfluous. From the antique lyre to modern lyric, from the construction of the pyramids to the erection of the Eiffel Tower.

And how does it show that people are unhappy precisely when they miss superfluous things? Well, people with full stomachs sitting on sofas and watching TV can suffer under depression even if they have more than enough to live on. People who take their own lives hardly do so out of starvation and thirst, but mostly because of unrequited love, out of conviction, euphoria, disappointment, or due to illness or despair. The fact that suicide is not on the decline but on the rise along with the overall standard of living speaks in favor of Ortega y Gasset's claim: For humans only the superfluous is necessary.

And basic income? Is basic income superfluous in this sense? Happily, no. It is unconditional and ensures the necessary. Can we get to the superfluous without the necessary? Of course not. So it would be wrong to misconstrue Ortega y Gasset as meaning that homeless people should be treated to a classical concert or the like. Not forcing people to their happiness with superfluous things is the goal of basic income, and instead building on the necessary in order to secure them the opportunity to take part in the superfluous.

"Even if the human being lives in a well-heated home and has plenty to eat, this is not yet the deciding factor in their worth. But they must live warmly and be well-fed if their better nature is to stir within them," writes Friedrich Schiller on November 11th, 1793 to the later Frederick Christian II, Duke of Schleswig-Holstein-Sonderburg-Augustenburg.[103] In Ortega y Gasset's terms, this means: Whereas our nature and technology provide for what we need, it is we ourselves who are at all times responsible for the superfluous. The human being is the entity that can only survive in abundance. For the human being, the superfluous is a necessity. This is a formula for freedom: Freedom begins beyond necessity.

Myself and the Other Animals

People who have a sense of the right direction but are still uncertain sometimes call for experimentation: How would people behave if they had an unconditional basic income? The answer to this question lies in the future. It involves the behavior of every individual human being, which is something that cannot be formalized or mathematically ascertained.

But there have indeed been experiments that shed light on the questions posed by basic income. In 1949, American psychology professor Harry F. Harlow gave puzzles to eight Rhesus monkeys. The object of the puzzles was to open a certain kind of lock. Harlow wanted to find out how monkeys learn. The predominant behaviorist doctrine of that time stated that primates only become active if food or reproduction is at stake—unless one takes great effort to teach them a certain behavioral pattern by rewarding them for "correct" behavior. To everyone's surprise, though, the monkeys solved Harlow's task without any reward and lost interest in the game when he gave them raisins in order to improve their performance. Harlow was so perplexed over the monkeys' behavior that he abandoned this line of investigation. He did write down, though, that what motivated the monkeys must be some kind of "third force," one beyond the urge to eat and reproduce.[104]

It was not until 20 years later that another researcher took up the questions raised by Harlow's experiment. American behavioral scientist Edward L. Deci repeated Harlow's monkey experiments, this time with humans. Deci gave the people in his test a kind of Rubik's cube and instead of raisins he rewarded them with money. The result confirmed the one Harlow had reached in 1949: The moment the test subjects were paid to solve the problem, they lost all desire to work at solving the puzzle for no reward. The money seemed to rob them of the pleasure they took in the activity itself.[105]

This also confirms a further study conducted by Deci, in which students were to solve puzzles in three sequential units. In the first unit they were to perform a task without any prior instructions. In the second unit, one group continued to play without instructions, while the other group was separated and paid for solving the puzzle. In the third unit, Deci had both groups play without any reward. The result: The students who had been paid in the second unit gave up trying to solve the puzzle after a much shorter time than their fellow students.[106]

Nowadays, the "third force" Harlow wrote about is known as intrinsic motivation. The questions raised by Harlow's and Deci's experiments are the very questions that basic income asks: Do we deprive ourselves of intrinsic motivation when we force ourselves to work? Does our work fulfill us only when we do it for its own sake and not in return for pay?

The most comprehensive experiment pertaining to basic income, one that can be repeated at any time, is the following survey: What work would you do if your income were taken care of? So far, hundreds of thousands of people have responded to this question. The result: positive. The overwhelming majority of the respondents would continue to work. Most of these would even go on doing what they are doing now. Many of them think they would be able to do the same thing even better. And no small amount of them think they would do the same thing but in another place, in a different business. It is worth noting that a great deal of the respondents desired change, a continuation of their education, and less pressure and stress.

What do you think the others would do if their income were taken care of? If we turn the question around, the result is negative. The same amount of respondents who say that they themselves would go on working believe that the others would stop working. We have an optimistic, human image of ourselves and a pessimistic, animal image of others. In the German economy magazine *brand eins*, the column "The World in Numbers" states: "Portion of people who assert that even with an unconditional basic income they would go on working: 90%. Portion of people who believe unconditional basic income would cause others to stop working: 80%."[107]

Unconditional basic income requires only a slight modification of the existing state of affairs: Guaranteeing unconditionally the portion of income that each individual needs in order to live. What, if you please, could possibly be so dangerous about that?

The human being is the entity who actually becomes what they think about themselves and others. You can prove this for yourself by means of the following little experiment: For a month, pay attention to the situations in which you make decisions based on securing your existence. Write this down. Write down as well how you would have decided if you had an unconditional basic income.

Once the month has passed, make a tentative evaluation: In what way would your life change if you had acted as if you had unconditional basic income? Would you be lazier? Or more productive? What effects would it have on the decisions you make and on your overall attitude toward life? What would be the consequences for your fellow human beings?

In the following month, observe how your life would change if the people in your life had an unconditional basic income. Would they be less stressed out? More approachable? More helpless? And what changes would these things cause in your own life?

In the third month, ask others what would change in their lives if they had an unconditional basic income. Write down the answers and think over how these changes would affect your own life. What advantages and disadvantages would there be for you? What opportunities and challenges? Begin with this experiment whenever you want.

Things Go Better Without Help

"I think unconditional basic income is an immoral concept,"[108] states Lukas Rühli, project manager of *avenir suisse*, a Swiss economic think tank. He justifies his claim as follows: "Especially as far as fairness is concerned, it seems most reasonable to me to help those people who cannot help themselves and to demand of people who can help themselves that they take care of their own lives."

What does this line of argumentation teach us? It is about morality, justice and helping. It is clear that Rühli sees unconditional basic income not as a fundamental right, but as a social benefit, as welfare assistance. He builds his entire argument on this presupposition.

To provide help is a fundamental human gesture. In the Middle Ages, monetary aid was provided in the form of alms. In many religions giving alms was even seen as an obligation. In the wake of the Enlightenment and the advent of the Industrial Age, personal charity was transformed into the political system of social security. Otto von Bismarck was a pioneer of the welfare state in the late 19th century, and even today we speak in terms of the Bismarckian welfare state. The Bismarckian welfare state signaled a large step in the development of society: The practice of helping the individual citizen became a political issue, and has since become established as the modern welfare state, along with its wide variety of different social benefits.

Whether brought about through supplication in medieval times or through political demand in modern times, providing aid to people in financial need is always about the relationship between the helper and the person receiving help. St. Martin is the model of a helper in the Middle Ages. He shares his coat with a beggar who has nothing and is unable to help himself. From 1957 through 1980, St. Martin graced the Swiss 100-Frank-note. It's a strong picture: Those people receive help who are unable to help themselves.

Lukas Rühli's argument runs along these lines. There are always people who fail, and there ought to be a safety net for them; it is a moral obligation to help them. Helping people who can help themselves, Rühli goes on to conclude, amounts to an encroachment on their private affairs: We would be helping people who don't need helping. They would be receiving an unconditional income for no reason. Even worse: The state would be inciting them to inactivity.

This is what we learn from Rühli's position: Help from the state supports a two-class society, the upper class consisting of the helpers and the lower class of those in need of help. Basic income cancels the two-class society: I don't need any help. I am fully capable of leading an independent and autonomous life. I no longer have to rely on help from others; that's over with. What helps me is not having to rely on help from others. If everyone receives a basic income, no one will have to come to anyone else's financial rescue. Swiss journalist Michael Sennhauser finds a fitting image for this: "If everyone is their own king, no one needs to be king over anyone else."[109]

We have gone from a noble-minded will to relieve others in need to a state-administered mechanism for upholding a relationship of dependency. We have institutionalized and perverted St. Martin. A perverted St. Martin shares not his coat, but his morals. One set of morals for the helpers and a different set for the needy.

Today, especially in Germany, need is not relieved, but taken advantage of. It is raw material for the poverty industry. "The unemployment business is booming. Monetary sums in the billions are vanishing into senseless one-euro-jobs and a monstrous bureaucracy," writes *Der Spiegel* concerning the German "benefits factory."[110] German entrepreneur Götz W. Werner designates the so-called Hartz-IV regime as an "open penal institution."[111] And Heribert Prantl, a chief editor at the German newspaper *Süddeutsche Zeitung*, laments: "With our benefit system, elements of penal law have found their way into social law. [...] This law treats people as potential loafers who need loafing driven out of them at every turn. [...] The dubious poisonous pedagogy, so frowned upon when it comes to raising children, is alive and well in the benefits system for the sake of disciplining adults."[112]

In more affluent Switzerland things are different, if no less dire. The Federal Statistical Office has ascertained that 60% of people legally eligible for welfare benefits do not claim them: Of the 586,000 people entitled to welfare payments in Switzerland in 2012, only 231,000 actually received welfare benefit payments. The main reasons for the high rate of non-payment of these benefits are doubt, shame, fear of debt, people's fear of altering their residency status, or their relatives' obligation to support them.[113]

Helping someone can make a person feel a sense of satisfaction. What nicer thing is there than being truly useful to people in need? Today we abuse this noble cause: We defame people as social parasites. The political answer to this state of affairs is the social detective, a calamity both for people willing to help and for those entitled to receive it.

Unconditional basic income liberates charity from its manipulative outgrowths. Whereas today I have to dress up as a beggar to receive support from a government that acts like St. Martin, basic income demands no more and no less of me than my self-determination. In today's social welfare system, I receive money for the wrong reason, whereas with basic income I have money for what is right.

In Lukas Rühli's opinion, it is fair for everyone to take care of themselves. It is, he claims, fair if everyone who can look after themselves must do so; and it is unfair if someone able to do so does not have to.[114] Unconditional basic income breaks the spell of this kind of morality: Yes, we can—if we don't have to.

People who Determine Themselves Liberate Others

Almost everyone thinks self-determination is a good thing. At least as long as there is a wise commander-in-chief to make sure that things don't go haywire. Total chaos seems a very real danger if everyone can do as they please.

The worry that self-determination might tip and turn into universal disgruntlement is based on wrong notions of self-determination. Self-determination does not mean that there are no longer any laws in force. Moreover, self-determination does not mean that we suspend the demands we make on others. Self-determination means that all the claims and needs I have, that all my wishes and hopes can only be meaningfully fulfilled if they are granted by other people who determine themselves. Self-determination is always others' self-determination. Only if I trust others to determine themselves am I in a position to achieve my own self-determination.

It's clear that I want to live a life that I determine for myself, there's no getting around that. But there needs to be someone to call the shots for the others so that everything goes in the right direction. This is the thought that makes me a slave of my own fear of living a self-determined life. Without others determining themselves, my own self-determination is bread without butter, a pipe dream, a lofty goal.

And who's in charge, assuming I really do determine myself? The others! That's what is so special about it: The self-determining person is not the one who refuses to meet others' demands, but the one better able to see these demands and freer to take them on. The self-determining person is not out to contradict everybody else. That is the self-determination phase of puberty, the phase of defiance. Self-determination is different: It is the possibility for me to connect with a task in the world of my own free will, and for me to grow through this connection. Today, all other ties break sooner or later, and no chief determiner is going to be able to change that.

We are afraid of self-determination because we still see the free individual as a troublemaker, an agitator, as someone who thinks they're better than the others. But whoever looks down on the free individual is only degrading themselves. They are using a stick called resentment to beat that part of their own nature that thinks they're better than the rest. Basic income invites each and every one of us to think we're something better. It lends us poise, which distinguishes us, not a relieving posture that debases us.

Anyone unwilling to count on self-determined people or wanting to appoint a commander-in-chief over them prefers a society of subordinates, compliant servants, assimilated beasts of burden. In the long run, that is the worst thing that can happen to us—us not producing people with the capacity for critical judgment, but assimilated, drained, ambitionless working corpses. If we want to master the challenges of the future, autonomy is our only chance. It is the only thing that provides the certainty that the people I am speaking with actually are people. If I turn to a person who is determined by others, they do not answer me as a human being, but as a machine, as a non-entity, as an absence. We aren't going to be able to afford that any longer if we want to go on being able to afford our humanity.

Only the Slave Who Becomes Master Is Free

Today we consider it a matter of course to concede civil rights to one another, among which are freedom of speech, free choice of domicile, free choice of profession, freedom of travel and of religion. If anyone is forced to belong to a certain religion or to practice a certain profession or to limit their mobility, we consider that unfair, even unworthy.

These rights to freedom are not something we may take for granted; far from it. They were only achieved during the Age of Enlightenment. What constituted the freedom of a Roman slave was the freedom of the slave owner to rent, sell or free them. But for a slave a life in freedom was unthinkable as long as they lacked property, the foundation necessary for their existence. No one without land had any claim to agricultural yield. Thus the slave owner guaranteed the slave's existence, which the latter earned by cultivating the owner's land. To release a slave without providing them with the possibility to make use of this freedom was not to release them, but to make them an outlaw. The only chance the slave had to make use of their freedom was either to find a new master or to go on serving the old one. Emancipation of a slave was oftentimes not an act of grace, but rather a delayed death penalty.[115]

Today we are connected with this picture in various ways. First: Slaves had basic needs that had to be met for them to be able to work at all. No dead slave was a good slave. And we have remained beings of need to this day. We are neither free nor unfree against these needs; it's just that our existence is endangered if they are not met. Only when my existence is guaranteed do I have questions that go beyond guaranteeing it.

Second: The work contract of a modern-day managed employee goes back to the law of tenancy to which slaves were subjected in Ancient Rome.[116] The master—whom today we call the employer—owes the employee a living. In an economy based on external supply, this living no longer consists in making land available for subsistence farming, but rather in providing money to enable the employee the purchase of goods and services. As long as this income is guaranteed along with the safety regulations the labor unions have stood up for so commendably over the past century and a half, the employer is entitled to use the employee to serve their—the employer's—goals and purposes. To be sure, since ancient times the employee has attained the status of a natural person and hence is subject to civil rights and obligations; nevertheless, the employer still disposes over their manpower and hence disposing over them as a beast of burden, the same as the Roman master over his slave, whom he was entitled to rent out, to sell or to destroy.

Third: The master took care of his underlings as head of the household and saw to it that they wanted what they were supposed to want. Living and working conditions were set up such that they had no choice but to do what they were supposed to. Since today in a society built around division of labor it is necessary to earn money in order to consume, the things we produce must necessarily make money. The only way to make oneself useful is by showing not obedience toward a master, but allegiance to the market. The master's hand was visible, but the hand of the market has become invisible. But both hands have a raised forefinger and proclaim the following threat: If you don't want what counts for us, we will withhold from you the things you need!

Now the question arises as to how we can set up our political and social circumstances in a way that civil liberties—from the freedom to choose one's own profession to that of speech—do not seem as cynical as the freedom granted to a liberated but penniless Roman slave. The answer couldn't be simpler: All we need to do is liberate the guarantee of a person's livelihood from the conditions that hamper this guarantee. Let's just grant everyone absolutely what they absolutely need. Why ought everyone be entitled to what they absolutely need? Because they need it absolutely! Any and all conditions attached to this need are inefficient. A guarantee on everyone's existence is the most efficient way to maintain society—because everyone receives it.

And what about the so-called dirty work? The notion of dirty work stems from an era when for the social elite all work was dirty, whereas for everyone else it was considered an unavoidable fact of life. On the farm the cows need to be milked, the crops harvested, the bread baked. The dignity of my doing this work derives from my acknowledgement that it needs doing—and simplifying, if possible. Today's dirty work is a specter wreaking havoc in many fellow human beings. It's hard to say just what work is dirty. Is it dirty to launder money? To wash the car? Or elderly people? Or dishes? And what work is clean?

There is no such thing as dirty work. There is nothing but work that somebody has to do and work that nobody has to. Today we indulge excessively in fake work that doesn't need doing, simply because so many jobs are no more than places to earn an income. And today our vision for work that needs doing is blurred, our view clouded by our fearing for our existence.

Unconditional basic income enables us a clear view on what we owe each other. It allows me to recognize what I can do for others, and it makes sure that the laws guaranteeing civil liberty do not deteriorate into sanctimonious clichés like the one about the emancipated Roman slave.

My Freedom Grows with Yours

How does my freedom relate to others' freedom? The established idea is: My freedom ends at the boundary of the other person's freedom. If I want to be freer, the other person has to become less free. If I want to be entirely free, I have to restrict or even suppress the other person's freedom. Otherwise, it poses a danger to my freedom. "Your freedom is far from equaling mine. / My freedom:

ja! Your freedom: *nein!,*" as cabaret artist Georg Kreisler sings about false freedom fantasies.[117]

Kreisler's critic of false freedom fantasies resembles musty living-room liberalism. It postulates self-realization within one's own four walls—or in the neighbors' living room, if I occupy it and feel free in their place. But this living room liberalism is long since obsolete. Today my freedom no longer leads to others' unfreedom. My unfreedom promotes unfreedom. My freedom promotes freedom.

Unfreedom reproduces itself. Say I am in favor of having the others monitored because I feel threatened by them and hope that monitoring them will increase my own safety. This hoped-for security will only make me feel all the more insecure. In my insecure need for security, everyone suddenly appears to me as a threat to my safety. I see my own insecurity in the eyes of everyone else. Not a trace of security any longer.

Today my freedom no longer threatens others' freedom; rather, freedom is a gift the others give me. Freedom is not indivisible; rather, freedom grows as it is shared. All the other people whose freedom I enable put me in a position to realize this freedom for myself as well. If I regard the others as unfree and consider only myself capable of freedom, this freedom of mine is nothing other than rebellion. Liberal selfishness.

As early as 1871, Norwegian author Henrik Ibsen wrote to Danish literary critic Georg Brandes: "He who possesses liberty otherwise than as an aspiration possesses it soulless, dead. One of the qualities of liberty is that, as long as it is being striven after, it goes on expanding. Therefore, the man who stands still in the midst of the struggle and says, 'I have it,' merely shows by so doing that he has just lost it."[118]

Today's freedom is a reciprocal mix. We regain it on a day-to-day basis by ensuring each other's existence, in this way grant-

ing each other what we need and mutually freeing one another for
our respective tasks in life.

If You Can't Coerce, You'll have to Convince

In a society built around basic income, purpose economy has the
advantage and profit economy has a handicap. Basic income bol-
sters the meaningfulness in an economy, because everyone is in on
deciding just what matters. Thus, thinking strictly in terms of
making profits loses its leverage, since no one has to take part who
doesn't want to.

Unconditional basic income is a thorn in the side of the
money-for-money economy. But basic income provides better
prerequisites for anyone who wishes to achieve something more
meaningful with their investment than the sheer turn of a profit.
The investor faces the question of who they want to be of service
to: If they want meaning, they will probably have to sacrifice
short-term profits. If they want fast and dirty money, they are
better served by going where there is no basic income. Their
chances of earning profits from inhumane conditions will definitely be stronger.

In 2015, the Edelman Trust Barometer showed that people
the world over place more trust in non-profit organizations. Anyone who does not work for a profit is less manipulable. And this is
just what people appreciate.[119]

If you can't coerce, you'll have to convince. If you want to
reduce fear and make people less susceptible to blackmail, you'll
have to guarantee safety and freedom. If on the other hand you
want to utilize others for your own purposes, you'll need to keep
them on a short leash. It is particularly effective to keep them in

line by means of little perks and by drawing their attention to the fact that others are even worse off than they are.

It is easy to earn profits in a system based on economic survival of the fittest. All you need is people whose income does not exceed the existential minimum. The middle class can distance itself from it, and the upper class can settle in on top of it.

For those at the bottom of the heap it is most important that they feel at fault for having caused their own situation, and that at the same time they believe they are going to rise into the ranks of the middle class at any moment. And if you belong to the middle class, you need right now to be thinking and feeling as if you were part of the elite. In Swiss referendums you can tell that this functions quite well: The majority of the Swiss population cast their votes as if they already belonged to the upper class. On their supposed way to the top they vote as if they had already made it there.

The system of economic competition stabilizes itself by helping those who can demonstrate their inability to help themselves. The people at the top give to the people at the bottom. If you draw an unconditional basic income you no longer have to turn your imploring gaze upward and beg for help. You don't have to make yourself compliant. You don't have to compete for your existence; you can compete entirely for excellence.

World Economy as Hospitality

People who are active voluntarily are more successful. Take someone who runs a restaurant, for instance: If you run your restaurant of your own free will and hence vigorously and enthusiastically, you have a considerable competitive edge. The quality of a restaurant drops the more extrinsically the restaurateur is motivated. This is most clearly noticeable within the interpersonal services: In merchandising, in caregiving, in education, everywhere where human interaction takes place, it is crucial for your success that you are able to derive a sense of meaning from your work.

The hospitality principle holds for the entire economy: Even if we never personally meet the guest, that is, the person who articulates a need, they are nevertheless the person we work for. Business economy is a kind of hospitality business. Providing for others' needs.

With basic income we sharpen our view for the true needs of others. If money is the only thing we are working for, our wages are what is most important to us. It is more important that people buy from us and less important what we sell, how our product is made up and whether or not the purchaser really makes use of it. And so it is with everything: The more dependent we are, the narrower our field of vision becomes. Our vision widens as our independence increases. Independence is a quality factor. Basic income leads to our not having to bear our own needs in mind so much and thus being able to be more attentive for other peoples' needs. Whoever looks into the world sees others. Whoever looks only at themselves sees nothing.

We live from others' efforts. The better they are, the better we live. How can we see to it that we live better? By seeing to the wellbeing of the people who work for us. We safeguard their wellbeing as long as we see to it that their working conditions do not obstruct their finding fulfillment in their work. If the technology we develop serves this purpose, both the others' wellbeing and our own will increase.

Whoever follows through on the hospitality business principle ultimately arrives at unconditional hospitality: "Pure and unconditional hospitality, hospitality itself, opens or is in advance open to someone who is neither expected nor invited, to whomever arrives as an absolutely foreign visitor, as a new arrival, nonidentifiable and unforeseeable, in short, wholly other," as French philosopher Jacques Derrida states.[120] Whoever is open for guests, not only feels at home at his own place, but also at strangers. He has a friendly manner with strangers, the premise to not live beside each other but truly together.

Freedom I

The German word for free time, *Freizeit*, goes back to the medieval concept of *freyzeyt*, which in the 1300s referred to "times of market peace," *Marktfriedenszeit*. *Marktfriedenszeit* protects the market's sellers and buyers from disturbances of all kinds, even from official measures such as summonses or arrests. *Freizeit* is part-time peace. *Freizeit* is special working time.[121]

Free time as we know it today originally occurs in 1823 in the work of German educator Friedrich Fröbel. Fröbel uses the term to designate the time allowed the pupils of his educational institute, "for the pursuit of their personal and individual needs."[122] The Duden German etymological dictionary contains *Freizeit* for the first time in 1929 and defines it as "time during which a person does not have to work."[123]

There are two ways in which the notion of free time shows up: On one hand in the softening and later the utter dissolution of authoritarian structures. Here, individualization creates new space for self-determined life styles. On the other hand, free time is a result of the industrial revolution and of the alienation of humans from what they do as caused by the division of labor. The industrial age, though, does not take us into factories and assembly lines only; it is rather the point of departure for unforeseen technological progress—resulting in an increase in productivity many times over. The key to this increase is energy production and the resulting mechanization and rationalization of labor. Estranged but effective. The development of agriculture is one particularly telling manifestation of this: In around 1900, a German farmer produced food for approximately four people. In 1949 he fed ten people; in 2004 he fed 127; and by 2012 this number had increased to 144.[124]

The notion of free time enters in when work and life are separated. When work is no longer done or wanted in a natural and self-evident way and instead people degenerate to cogs in a giant machine, the thought occurs that they need some free time.

Speaking of free time only makes sense relative to a job that someone does not do voluntarily; to forced labor, so to speak, that one pursues because one has to. Wherever work is experienced not as meaningful activity, but as drudgery and a necessary evil, people want not only pay as compensation, but rights as well, which guarantee a life other than the person's work life. We owe it to the labor unions and to social democracy that their struggle in the field of labor has led to less working time, better pay and more free time.

20th century capitalists were more or less recognizant of the demands for improved working conditions. By salami technique, the working class was gradually granted more free time. After all, the workers needed to recover from the strain of their work in order to return to their jobs with renewed strength.

In the workers' eyes free time is earned compensation. I have free time; therefore, I am. I work; therefore, I am entitled to free time. Time during which I do not have to work. Time during which I can determine for myself what I do. Time during which I do not have to follow orders.

I am compensated for my work effort, and while on the job I am bound by the instructions and expectations of my employer. I sell my manpower, my life time. I can decide for myself what I do with the wages I receive. Inasmuch as this is so, I am free: freedom I.

Freedom II

People who do not do what they want to do have to be made to want what they are supposed to do. In the emerging capitalist industrialism, workinghouses and reformatories were instituted with this end in mind. Their purpose is to guarantee people's willingness to work by training their inmates to observe such old-school virtues as punctuality, diligence and orderliness. Control over those who do not participate in the system of gainful employment can be traced back to this tradition, as can the restrictions imposed by the bureaucracy of the welfare system, replete with its bureaucratic language, which is a relic from the Wilhelminian Era.

This legacy from the early modern age could be alleviated by means of basic income: It would be in the hands of each individual to decide how they want to live. The bloated administrative bureaucracy—which to this day sees to disciplinary measures against those who allegedly refuse to contribute to the overall work effort—could simply be eliminated.

At all events, basic income would permit a different approach to time management. On this topic, German social psychologist Harald Welzer writes: "While today working hours are the only time that is considered to be spent in a functionally meaningful way, in an era of modern sustainability both time spent doing everyday chores and time spent doing nothing at all could be considered equally valid, because the sovereignty over a person's time would be transferred more to the single person and to their particular needs and preferences."[125] According to Welzer, time could to a much greater degree become a person's own self-determined time. It is high time for that, says Swiss philosopher Stephan Brotbeck: "We need more leisure in order not to become zombies."[126]

Leisure means being able to live in a self-determined way not just during our free time. In times to come, endowing our working time with meaning will become more and more crucial. I no longer want just to carry out things that others have thought out. I want to be able to take part in the thinking process, in the management process, in the responsibility; in this way I can take my own self-development, my own self-unfolding in hand while I am performing my work.

150 years ago and more, the Industrial Revolution enabled considerable advances in rationalization and gains in efficiency. But in recent decades the process of digitalization has enabled an exponential increase in the possibilities of rationalization and heightened efficiency. Digitalization leads to change not just in factories, but in numerous vocational fields as well. Anything that can be calculated can also be automated. This pertains as much to cashiers as it does to bankers, and will soon even apply to motor vehicle drivers.

The limits of rationalization are those of the human being. Soon, the only things not subject to automation will be the things people take up under their own self-leadership, not the prescribed tasks that people carry out. The professions of the future will only be possible where people have to think for themselves and not where calculations are run. Humans are needed less than ever to execute applications and combinations. But for everything of a creative and self-responsible nature, humans are becoming all the more necessary. This trend will make the notion of free time obsolete and lead to its discontinuation. Free time is based on the presupposition that there are other times during which I give up my freedom.

"People who really work cannot get enough of it," writes Swiss author Ludwig Hohl.[127] "Truly active people are incapable of overexerting themselves. The only way people can overexert themselves is by engaging in the wrong activity or in an unfulfilling one, one that begins to show flaws."[128] I need free time when a job begins to prove flawed because it is not really my job.

As far as my work is concerned, it leads me to myself and strengthens me. I do not want to be liberated from work; I want to be liberated within it: freedom II.

Commitment Through Freedom

We endeavor to create freedom by making detailed specifications and establishing sophisticated work parameters. But isn't this approach outdated? To frame the question differently: When do rules create freedom?

Questions pertaining to freedom will always require renegotiation from time to time. Speed limits restrict our freedom to drive as fast as we want, but they also give us the freedom to move about in traffic with greater certainty. Speed limits on public streets create the freedom to drive with greater safety. The same holds for food legislation, which prescribes hygiene standards, implements effective inspection of foodstuffs and promotes training and education throughout the entire field of food production and consumption.

Freedom is more than less government. It is the government's task to enable individual freedom through meaningful regulations. Unconditional basic income guarantees this: It leads to a free space that the state guarantees for each individual to lead their own life. At the same time, it leads to a reduction of government influence on the life of the individual.

When does freedom generate commitment? When it is more than just the freedom to choose the lesser of two evils. When it is freedom of production and not just of consumption. Basic income creates more freedom of production, more freedom to decide how and why I wish to become involved as a human being and in what way and to what extent I want to be active. With a basic income I have a guaranteed basis on which to become active. My need for money is no longer a reason for me to become dense; instead, it is solid ground under my feet. I can cut loose. I am more at liberty to think over what I want to do; more at liberty to think over where I might be needed.

Failure for Experts

If a recipient of unconditional basic income fails, it is because of themselves and not because of the missing basis. Failure is no longer a threat to our existence; instead, it exhausts itself within the task at hand. Basic income does not eliminate failure; it rather creates a human foundation for the sake of productive failure. If we are to learn from failure, it must be impossible for us to perish from it. What's the use of failing if there's nothing for me to learn from it?

Basic income makes us better able to learn from our mistakes. The capacity to commit errors is one of the most important prerequisites to innovation. Anyone afraid of failure ventures nothing and falls into inactivity. Obviously, not all manure is suitable as fertilizer, but without any manure at all there would be no fertilizer either.

People who learn from their mistakes have a feeling of exhilaration. But to deduce from this that we need to create circumstances intentionally under which people are guaranteed to fail is to draw a fatal conclusion. Everyone is capable of failing for themselves. Anyone who hinders this by intentionally causing others to fail impedes innovation.

Basic income is a safety net. It is possible to fall without falling through the net. It's like setting anchors when mountain climbing: Anchoring makes it possible to climb mountains that we would otherwise not dare to climb. Anchoring helps us feel sure that we will not fall in case we make a mistake. The key thing is that the safety line is not used only after an accident has already happened, but beforehand. And: Everyone is roped up, including the mountain guide; even those who have never had a mishap before.

Unconditional basic income is neither a reward nor a penalty. It is not a training instrument either. It does, however, make self-education possible by lifting the taboo on failure.

An error-friendly society is more flexible and successful that one that condemns error. This is why it makes sense to hang out a friendly net for errors. To fail is human. Failure that deprives us of our existential basis is inhumane. Unconditional basic income reduces the drop height of failure. It allows us to fall and makes it possible for us to get up again.

The Dance of Freedom

What is leadership? How can people be led? How can leadership be justified? Leadership today can no longer have any goal other than people leading themselves. Any leadership that wants anything else discredits itself. Any leadership that does not strive to lead to self-leadership abuses all those it leads. Leadership leaves people free to the extent that it seeks to render itself redundant. If it does not do this, it acts in the service of dependency.

The question is: What does leadership serve, freedom or dependency? Take the tango dance, for instance. The man leads the woman. One might conclude from this that the man is the one calling the shots. But that would be quite wrong. The gentleman leads the lady in service of the movement. He does not say what she is supposed to do; rather, he provides the space for her to move. It's about subtle interaction.

The ultimate experience for the female partner is to give herself over entirely to her male counterpart, to unite with and savor the maneuvering-room he provides her. She goes along with him utterly, but without denying herself. Giving oneself up in the process of giving oneself over is unattractive. So is holding back for the sake of asserting one's autonomy. Being aloof is not the same as being autonomous.

The magic word that connects dance partners is trust. Those female dancers are the most sought after who trustingly give themselves over without giving themselves up. They are the ones who make it possible for the male dance partners to go beyond themselves. Women who do not trust their dance partners cause them to freeze and to grow two left feet. And something similar happens to female dance partners led by untrusting men and by male partners who have a false understanding of what it means to lead. They cannot give themselves over if the male partner wants to be everything or nothing. They stumble over his legs or step on other dancers' feet.

Leadership in the service of others' movement. Giving oneself over without giving oneself up. Such are the challenges of Argentine tango dancing. If two dancers are skillful, it is impossible to tell who is leading and who is following. Each partner leads the other into free spaces they could never have entered without the other. Leadership becomes research of free spaces.

In former times being able to get people to do things was considered a success. This is how the Egyptian pyramids and the Eiffel Tower came about. In the future, success will consist in enabling others to become active in a self-responsible way. Good teachers aren't the ones who know better; they're the ones who serve their students. Good bosses aren't the ones who command the personnel; they are the ones who serve their human resources. Good politicians aren't the ones who represent themselves; they're the ones who serve their voters.

Freedom is an ardent dance. Freedom does not mean being untouchable. It means being able to connect with others. Freedom can be neither bought nor prescribed. But it can be made possible by promoting self-leadership and self-responsibility.

Until now, freedom was always gained by fighting or by working one's way toward it. First it was emancipation from nature, then from absolute rulership, finally the attainment of civil rights, the revival of democracy, the struggle for better working conditions, the emancipation of women and the free-market economy. In times to come, freedom will not so much have to be fought for, as taken hold of.

Formerly, our social coherency was determined by external structures. The circumstances we were born into were our guides. Blood relations carried us, but they also held us captive. Authoritarian systems were a given. It never occurred to a servant that they could be a master. We have freed ourselves from this and become individuals. Freedom is for each individual person.

The future is the presence of free connections. Relationships of our own choice are gaining in importance. People who raise themselves above others will end up as underdogs. Those who seek to exploit others will lose out. Those who place their freedom at the service of others can hear the dance music of the future.

What's Next

Why don't we have an unconditional basic income yet? Because we are still unwilling to let go the idea that the others have to do something to secure their own existence. Because we want to force them to do something to secure their own existence. Because we are still unwilling to grant others the very self-responsibility we claim for ourselves.

Unconditional basic income is no revolution. Earlier, we fetched water at the village well. Today there are water faucets everywhere where water is needed. When the idea was born to lay water pipes, the misgivings were considerable: We won't meet each other at the well anymore. Our togetherness is going to fall apart. And I ask you: Who is going to make sure that everybody else turns off the water faucets, and that nobody misuses them? Once basic income has been implemented, it will be just as much a matter of fact as water faucets are today.

Unconditional basic income is not an added frill; it is letting go of superfluous stipulations. It lets possibilities run free. People unable to control themselves tend to want to control others. Basic income promotes self-control.

*   *   *

Democracy is an ongoing meeting to debate the question of priorities. There are two factors that work in tandem on this: The bindingness of the laws in force and the possibility for these laws to be questioned and altered time and again. The preservation of justice and the shaping of it are democracy's kindred partners.

The Swiss popular initiative for an unconditional basic income asks just what it is that speaks against ensuring people's existence with no strings attached: Do we become lazy or liberated? Dangerous or docile? Motivated or fainthearted?

On the Sunday evening of the constitutional referendum, two graphs will be visible on the television screen: one for the yesses and one for the nos. Some people will have voted "yes" for a good reason, and a definitely larger number will, for various reasons, have said "no." Most of these, while they will have their doubts, will nevertheless want to think the matter further: Yes, but who's going to do all the dirty work? Yes, but how do we finance it? Yes, but won't it eliminate the welfare state? Yes, but who's going to do vocational training? Yes, but aren't we going to be flooded by foreigners? Yes, but isn't it unfair? The best "yes" is the one in favor of thinking the matter further.

Popular initiatives don't need to be accepted to be successful. When in 1989 Switzerland voted on whether to abolish the army, the 36% approval rate signaled the beginning of the end of the Swiss army. Before that, a career in the army was the prerequisite to advancement in the business world and in society. Since then, it seems more like anyone unable to do without a career in the military has a problem with authority. The popular initiative caused a fundamental change in the army because it revealed that more than every third Swiss citizen was willing even to do away with it. The fall of the Berlin Wall in 1989 contributed to this change as well.

What conceptual wall will fall to enable the introduction of unconditional basic income? Will it be work that can no longer be made possible otherwise? Will it be the purchasing power that can no longer be guaranteed otherwise? Will it be the sustainability that can no longer be maintained otherwise? At all events, unconditional basic income will come not for moral reasons, but for pragmatic ones. At the latest, it will come when nothing else works anymore.

*   *   *

We normally speak of a utopia when someone suggests something we either do not want or cannot envision. People who suggest things want to change something. And people who do not want this change are quick at hand with the word utopia, in order to defend the status quo. That is a contradiction. If something is genuinely utopic, thus incapable of being carried out, there is no need to defend oneself against it. All a person need do is observe it, free of fear and without any qualms. If unconditional basic income were a utopia, no one would be fighting it.

The popular initiative for an unconditional basic income suggests guaranteeing a portion of the income that everyone needs in order to live. Anyone who makes what is unconditional contingent on conditions is inept. It is unwise to allow lack and shortage to predominate in the midst of abundance, and to allow bondage to predominate in a free society.

Unconditional basic income demands nothing. It is not a matter of more for some and less for others. It is a matter of securing what secures everyone. No basic income is a utopia.

Appendix

FAQ about the Constitutional Referendum

What, exactly, is on the ballot of the popular initiative for an unconditional basic income?

A vote will be taken on June 5th, 2016 to add the following article to the Swiss Federal Constitution:

Art. 110a (new) Unconditional Basic Income
1. The Federation will see to the implementation of an unconditional basic income.
2. This basic income is to grant the entire population a humane existence and the participation in public life.
3. The law will regulate the financing of the basic income and the amount in which it is to be disbursed.

What is unconditional basic income?

Unconditional basic income is a fundamental right. It guarantees that part of the income that everyone needs in order to live. As a fundamental right it is provided without requiring either service in return or means testing.

Who receives unconditional basic income?

Unconditional basic income is disbursed to the entire population of a country, hence to all those who are legal residents of the country.

How high is the unconditional basic income?

Unconditional basic income makes possible a life in human dignity and enables full participation in public life. Calculations in Switzerland assume 2500 Swiss Franks per month for each adult, less for children. The exact amount is to be determined by political process.

How is unconditional basic income delivered?

The way unconditional basic income is delivered remains to be determined. Either it is to be levied directly, according to the amount of money spent (as consumption tax), or indirectly, according to money earned (as income tax). One way or another, it will show up as a cost component in existing prices.

How is unconditional basic income to be financed?

Monetarily, the financing of unconditional basic income is a zero-sum game. Since everyone will receive an unconditional basic income, existing incomes will drop in principle, according to the amount of basic income. Accordingly, the income costs paid for by the government and by business enterprises will drop by the amount set for basic income. Total expenses will remain the same, since the taxes through which basic income is financed will rise accordingly.

How much will unconditional basic income cost?

As things are, everyone today disposes over a conditional basic income; otherwise they could not stay alive. What is new about the unconditional basic income is that it is unconditional. It costs not more money, but trust. If everyone were to become inactive on account of unconditional basic income, there would be no long-term way to finance it. The actual financing question is as follows: What influences will the unconditional guarantee on our existence have on our activity?

An example from the field

Let's assume a typical monthly income in Switzerland of 7500 Swiss Franks. With basic income, this income would be made up in the following manner: 2500 Swiss Franks in basic income, 5000 Swiss Franks earned from gainful employment. The gross income of 7500 Swiss Franks would remain the same.

The national economic context

The volume of all the basic income in Switzerland totals around 200 billion Swiss Franks per year. That corresponds to roughly one-third the gross domestic product. Of these 200 billion Swiss Franks, 130 billion of the existing earned income can be transformed into basic income. The remaining 70 billion Swiss Franks are currently existing government transfer incomes that can be made unconditional by their transformation into basic income.

Glossary of Misconceptions

Wages for Everyone

Wages are remuneration for work performance. Unlike all forms of wages, unconditional basic income is not bound to any activity in return. It is unconditional. It is not remuneration of any kind. Wages are what a person earns in return for gainful employment. Unconditional basic income is what a person needs in order to perform work of any kind.

Money for Nothing

The notion that unconditional basic income is there in order not to work is erroneous. Basic income liberates people for work, for becoming involved, for taking initiative. The error is based on the assumption that work is no more than a compulsory measure. According to this fallacy we do nothing as long as we are not forced to. Unconditional basic income does not deprive us of our work motivation; our work motivation much rather increases by basic income preventing us from having to take bullshit jobs in order to survive.

More Money

Unconditional basic income is not an additional income; it is a fundamental one. If basic income were an additional income, it would be utopic. Just that is what a lot of people think: great idea; too bad it isn't financeable. Unconditional basic income frees all existing income within the range of the existential minimum from conditions. It unconditionally grants the base sum of already existing forms of income. This pertains to earned income as well as to government and private transfer income. Thanks to unconditional basic income, the only people who end up having more money are those who have less than the basic income in their bank accounts, or those who are underpaid for the gainful employment they pursue. The improved capacities to consume and to work with basic income will bring worthwhile returns on this investment.

Less Welfare State
Unconditional basic income does not do away with the welfare state. It replaces all existing social benefits in their present amount. The idea of lowering all social benefits to the level of basic income is a neoliberal ploy that social democrats fall for. They're afraid basic income might jeopardize their earnings in the amount of the existing social benefits. However, the exact opposite is the case: Unconditional basic income structures social benefits more independently by expanding them to include self-determination.

Only for Good People
According to one widespread misconception, unconditional basic income is for good people only, as it presupposes an idealistic image of what a human being is. But since—so the misconception continues—humans are not exclusively good, the idea of basic income, good though it may be, is unrealistic. This misguided notion is based on the further, underlying misconception that it is irresponsible to guarantee someone's existence without their doing something good in return. It inverts the entire intent of basic income: We as a society are not responsible for the errors and flaws of the individual; we are much rather responsible for others being able to make mistakes without these mistakes costing them their livelihood. Basic income does not presuppose good human beings; rather, it makes it possible for the good in every single human being to manifest.

Nobody does the Dirty Work

And who's going to do all the dirty work? This is a lot of people's favorite question, one that occurs in a broad palette of variations: Wouldn't unconditional basic income provide wrong work incentives? Why would anyone want to go on working if they had a basic income? Who works of their own free will, anyway? What all these variations have in common is that the respective question is not a question at all, but rather a claim disguised as a question. The true question is this: What is it that makes work dirty in the first place? The fact that it gets rid of dirt? The fact that we don't pay it well enough? That we don't appreciate it? What's dirty is not the work, but its circumstances. Basic income exposes this. Basic income cleans up the dirty work.

Danger of Inflation

Anyone who thinks basic income is an additional income rather than a fundamental one is at the same time afraid that it would lead to inflation. But since the principle of basic income is that the individual receives not more income, but an unconditional one, there is no way for it to cause an increase either in people's incomes or in the prices they pay. In certain individual cases, prices and incomes may indeed rise, but only those that are too low in the first place. Similarly, those incomes and prices that are too high will fall.

Redistribution Instrument

Time and again, the wish—or, as the case may be, the dread—comes up that with the help of unconditional basic income a redistribution of the wealth between the rich and the poor might occur. Basic income neither fulfills the wish nor does it provide any grounds for the dread. It does not redistribute money; what it redistributes is power. It empowers everyone not to have to bow down before the power of money.

Only Worldwide Implementation

Not infrequently, one hears the objection that it would be immoral to implement unconditional basic income in affluent Switzerland as long as there are other countries that are doing worse, not to mention the millions of people starving all over the world. To be sure, it is a travesty to be worried about luxury problems here as long as acute existential need holds sway in other parts of the world. All the same, it is a false objection against basic income. It will obviously not resolve the problem of world hunger if basic income is introduced in Switzerland. Nevertheless, the notion of refraining from doing a good thing on the grounds that it is not done somewhere else is short-sighted. Basic income helps heal this short-sightedness and helps broaden people's view for what is missing elsewhere.

Migration Incentive

Won't all the foreigners come if basic income comes? No. The right to immigrate is regulated by Swiss immigration law. The question of migration has nothing to do with basic income; the motives for migration have less to do with the possibilities the foreign country offers than with the impossibilities within the respective migrants' homeland.

Parenting Wage

There must be some hitch to someone simply getting money with no strings attached. There is no such thing as a free lunch. So what's the hitch on unconditional basic income? Some say it's a parenting wage, that is, money intended to re-chain the emancipated housewife to the kitchen. This fear is unfounded. Basic income is placed into the hand of the individual unconditionally. This individual is the one to decide what they want. Others say basic income is hush money that people draw in return for keeping their mouths shut, a kind of money pill to keep us quiet and docile. This too is absurd. Unconditional basic income is not hush money, but money for finding one's own voice.

Thanks

Our thanks go to Jules Ackermann, Joseph F. Bailey, Selma Bausinger, Ralph Boes, Kim-Fabian von Dall'Armi, Peter Dellbrügger, Stefan Heinrich Ebner, Tobias Faust, Arabelle Frey, Lilia I. Galarza Orcada, Daniel Graf, Deborah Grünwaldt, Nigel Grünwaldt, Niko Hammann, Tobias Handorf, Georg Hasler, Benjamin Hohlmann, Alexander Höhne, Johannes Jansen, Christine Kovce, Mikael Krogerus, Katrin Kruse, Andreas Laudert, Stephan Meyer, Ulrich Muchenberger, Christian Müller, Johanna Niermann, Claire Niggli, Esther Petsche, Ursula Piffaretti, Pola Elena Rapatt, Alma Rau, Konstantin J. Sakkas, Enno Schmidt, Veronika Sellier, Oswald Sigg, Alex Silber, Regula Stämpfli, Armin Steuernagel, Daniel Straub, Philippe Van Parijs, Troy Vine, Che Wagner, Theo Wehner, Albert Wenger, Götz W. Werner, Susanne Wiest, Marilola Wili, Benjamin Worel and all the others.

References

Anthony B. Atkinson (1995): Public Economics in Action: The Basic Income/Flat Tax Proposal. Oxford: Clarendon Press.

Peter Barnes (2014): With Liberty and Dividends for All: How to Save Our Middle Class When Jobs Don't Pay Enough. San Francisco: Berrett-Koehler.

Simon Birnbaum (2012): Basic Income Reconsidered: Social Justice, Liberalism, and the Demands of Equality. New York: Palgrave Macmillan.

Rutger Bregman (2016): Utopia for Realists: The Case for a Universal Basic Income, Open Borders, and a 15-hour Workweek. Amsterdam: The Correspondent.

Richard K. Caputo (ed.) (2012): Basic Income Guarantee and Politics: International Experiences and Perspectives on the Viability of Income Guarantee. New York: Palgrave Macmillan.

Charles M. A. Clark (2002): The Basic Income Guarantee: Ensuring Progress and Prosperity in the 21st Century. Dublin: The Liffey Press.

John Cunliffe, Guido Erreygers (eds.) (2004): The Origins of Universal Grants: An Anthology of Historical Writings on Basic Capital and Basic Income. New York: Palgrave Macmillan.

Sarath Davala, Renana Jhabvala, Soumya Kapoor Mehta, Guy Standing (2015): Basic Income: A Transformative Policy for India. London, New Delhi, New York & Sydney: Bloomsbury Academic.

Tony Fitzpatrick (1999): Freedom and Security: An Introduction to the Basic Income Debate. New York: Palgrave Macmillan.

Loek Groot (2010): Basic Income, Unemployment and Compensatory Justice. Boston: Kluwer Academic Publishers.

Sally Lerner, Charles M. A. Clark, W. Robert Needham (1999): Basic Income: Economic Security for All Canadians. Toronto: Between the Lines.

Rubén Lo Vuolo (ed.) (2013): Citizen's Income and Welfare Regimes in Latin America: From Cash Transfers to Rights. New York: Palgrave Macmillan.

Jennifer Mays, Greg Marston, John Tomlinson (eds.) (2016): Basic Income in Australia and New Zealand: Perspectives from the Neoliberal Frontier. New York: Palgrave Macmillan.

Ailsa McKay (2005): The Future of Social Security Policy: Women, Work and A Citizens Basic Income. London & New York: Routledge.

Matthew C. Murray, Carole Pateman (eds.) (2012): Basic Income Worldwide: Horizons of Reform. New York: Palgrave Macmillan.

Guinevere Liberty Nell (ed.) (2013): Basic Income and the Free Market: Austrian Economics and the Potential for Efficient Redistribution. New York: Palgrave Macmillan.

Daniel Raventós (2007): Basic Income: The Material Conditions of Freedom. London & Ann Arbor: Pluto Press.

Allan Sheahen (2012): Basic Income Guarantee: Your Right to Economic Security. New York: Palgrave Macmillan.

Maximilian Sommer (2016): A Feasible Basic Income Scheme for Germany: Effects on Labor Supply, Poverty, and Income Inequality. Heidelberg, New York, Dordrecht & London: Springer.

Guy Standing (ed.) (2004): Promoting Income Security as a Right: Europe and North America. London: Anthem Press.

Guy Standing, Michael Samson (eds.) (2003): A Basic Income Grant for South Africa. Cape Town: Juta Academic.

Andy Stern (2016): Raising the Floor: How a Universal Basic Income Can Renew Our Economy and Rebuild the American Dream. New York: PublicAffairs.

Malcolm Torry (2016): The Feasibility of Citizen's Income. New York: Palgrave Macmillan.

Malcolm Torry (1988): A Basic Income for All: A Christian Social Policy. Nottingham: Grove Books.

Yannick Vanderborght, Toru Yamamori (eds.) (2014): Basic Income in Japan: Prospects for a Radical Idea in a Transforming Welfare State. New York: Palgrave Macmillan.

Robert van der Veen, Loek Groot (eds.) (2000): Basic Income on the Agenda: Policy Objectives and Political Chances. Amsterdam: Amsterdam University Press.

Philippe Van Parijs (2001): What's Wrong with a Free Lunch? Boston: Beacon Press.

Philippe Van Parijs (1995): Real Freedom for All: What (if anything) Can Justify Capitalism? Oxford: Clarendon Press.

Philippe Van Parijs (ed.) (1992): Arguing for Basic Income: Ethical Foundations for a Radical Reform. London & New York: Verso.

Mark Walker (2016): Free Money for All: A Basic Income Guarantee Solution for the 21st Century. New York: Palgrave Macmillan.

Tony Walter (1989): Basic Income: Freedom from Poverty, Freedom from Work. London & New York: Marion Boyars Publishers.

Karl Widerquist (2013): Independence, Propertylessness, and Basic Income: A Theory of Freedom as the Power to Say No. New York: Palgrave Macmillan.

Karl Widerquist, Michael W. Howard (eds.) (2012): Alaska's Permanent Fund Dividend: Examining its Suitability as a Model. New York: Palgrave Macmillan.

Karl Widerquist, Michael W. Howard (eds.) (2012): Exporting the Alaska Model: Adapting the Permanent Fund Dividend for Reform around the World. New York: Palgrave Macmillan.

Karl Widerquist, José A. Noguera, Yannick Vanderborght, Jurgen De Wispelaere (eds.) (2013): Basic Income: An Anthology of Contemporary Research. Oxford: Wiley-Blackwell.

Erik Olin Wright (ed.) (2006): Redesigning Distribution: Basic Income and Stakeholder Grants as Cornerstones for an Egalitarian Capitalism. London & New York: Verso.

Notes

[1] Ludwig Hohl: Die Notizen oder Von der unvoreiligen Versöhnung, Frankfurt 1984, p. 32.

[2] Cf. Jean Ziegler: Wir lassen sie verhungern. Die Massenvernichtung in der Dritten Welt, Munich 2013.

[3] Cf. Georges Bataille: Das theoretische Werk I: Die Aufhebung der Ökonomie, Munich 1975.

[4] Peter Sloterdijk: Laudatio für Götz W. Werner anlässlich seiner Aufnahme in die Hall of Fame des Manager Magazins, 06/13/2012, URL: http://www.unternimm-die-zukunft.de/media/medialibrary/2012/06/laudatio_sloterdijk.pdf (05/30/2015).

[5] Cf. Deutsches Institut für Wirtschaftsforschung: Chinas Wirtschaft—Wie geht es weiter?, DIW Wochenbericht, no. 41/2013, URL: http//www.diw.de/documents/publikationen/73/diw_01.c.429028.de/ 13-41.pdf (05/30/2015).

[6] Cf. Bundesamt für Statistik: Sparquote privater Haushalte, 09/03/2013, URL: http://www.bfs.admin.ch/bfs/portal/de/index/themen/00/09/blank/ind42.indicator.420004.420001.html (05/30/2015).

[7] Rolf Zimmerman: "Vollbeschäftigung bleibt das Ziel," Die Wochenzeitung, no. 16/2012, URL: https://www.woz.ch/-29e1 (05/30/2015).

[8] Cf. Lutz Haverkamp: Angela Merkel erklärt Vollbeschäftigung zum politischen Ziel, Der Tagesspiegel, 09/09/2013, URL: http://www.tagesspiegel.de/politik/ardwahlarena-angela-merkel-erklaert-vollbeschaeftigung-zum-politischen-ziel/8765294 (05/30/2015).

[9] Jeremy Rifkin: "Wir verlieren unsere Arbeit an Maschinen," The European, no. 1/2015, URL: http://www.theeuropean.de/jeremy-rifkin/9333-die-zukunft-der-arbeitswelt (05/30/2015).

[10] Cf. Joachim Laukenmann: Menschheit steht vor dem größten Umbruch seit der industriellen Revolution, Sonntagszeitung, no. 1/2015, URL: http//www.sonntagszeitung.ch/read/sz_04_01_2015/gesellschaft/Menschheit-steht-vor-dem-groessten-Umbruch-seit-der-industriellen-Revolution-23180 (05/30/2015).

[11] Jeremy Rifkin: The End of Work: The Decline of the Global Labor Force and the Dawn of the Post-Market Era, New York 1995, p. 235.

[12] Robert Solow: Arbeit ohne Ende, The European, no. 3/2013, URL: http://www.theeuropean.de/robert-solow/7088-angst-vor-der-automatisierung-der-arbeit (05/30/2015).

[13] Theo Wehner, Sascha Liebermann: "Das bedingungslose Grundeinkommen macht nicht faul," Zeit Online, 12/30/2011, URL: http://www.zeit.de/politik/deutschland/2011-12/bedingungsloses-grundeinkommen-interview (05/30/2015).

[14] Cf. The Economist: The next supermodel, 02/02/2013, URL: http://www.economist.com/news/leaders/21571136-politicians-both-right-and-left-could-learn-nordic-countries-next-supermodel (05/30/2015).

[15] Cf. Jürgen Hoffmann, Roboter erobern deutsche Haushalte, Spiegel Online, 04/06/2013, URL: http://www.spiegel.de/wirtschaft/robotik-roboter-erobern-haushalte-a-888178.html (05/30/2015).

[16] Cf. Sandra Schulz: Paro, der Glücklichmach-Roboter, Spiegel Online, 10/24/2006, URL: http://www.spiegel.de/panorama/gesellschaft/pluesch-tech-fuer-senioren-paro-der-gluecklichmach-roboter-a-443593.html (05/30/2015).

[17] 2 Thessalonians 3:10.

[18] Cf. Götz W. Werner: Einkommen für alle. Der dm-Chef über die Machbarkeit des bedingungslosen Grundeinkommens, Cologne 2007, pp. 60f.

[19] Bertolt Brecht: Die Dreigroschenoper, Frankfurt 1968, p. 70.

[20] Cf. André Gorz: Paths to Paradise: On the Liberation from Work, London & Ann Arbor 1985.

[21] Cf. Helmut Gold (ed.): Wer nicht denken will, fliegt raus. Joseph Beuys Postkarten, Heidelberg 1998.

[22] Wassily Leontief: Input-Output-Economics, New York 1986, p. 372.

[23] Cf. Claudia Aebersold: Zahnpastaverkäufer und Philanthrop, Neue Zürcher Zeitung, 01/12/2014, URL: http://www.nzz.ch/wirtschaft/zahnpastaverkaeufer-und-philanthrop-1.18219733 (05/30/2015).

[24] Cf. Hannah Arendt: The Human Condition, Chicago & London 1958, p. 5.

[25] Cf. Steve Denning: Is Montessori the Origin of Google & Amazon?, Forbes, 02/08/2011, URL: http://www.forbes.com/sites/stevedenning/2011/08/02/is-montessori-the-origin-of-google-amazon/ (05/30/2015).

[26] Cf. Daniel H. Pink: Drive: The Surprising Truth About What Motivates Us, New York 2009.

[27] Cf. Uri Gneezy, Aldo Rustichini: Pay Enough or Don't Pay at All, Quarterly Journal of Economics, no. 115/2000, pp. 791-810, URL: http://pages.uoregon.edu/harbaugh/Readings/Misc%20experimental/gneezy%202000%20QJE%20pay%20enough.pdf (05/30/2015).

[28] Cf. Matthias Benz, Bruno S. Frey: The value of doing what you like. Evidence from the self-employed in 23 countries, Journal of Economic Behavior & Organization, no. 68/2008, p. 445-4558, URL: http://www.hanley.wiso.uni-kiel.de/downloads/seminar-2014/seminar_benz_sme.pdf (05/30/2015).

[29] Matthew 4:4.

[30] Karl-Martin Dietz: Führung: Was kommt danach? Perspektiven einer Neubewertung von Arbeit und Bildung, Karlsruhe 2011, p. 32.

[31] Cf. Wolfgang Brückner: "Arbeit macht frei." Herkunft und Hintergrund der KZ-Devise, Opladen 1998.

[32] Cf. Arena: Geld für alle: Vision oder Spinnerei? Schweizer Fernsehen SRF, 04/27/2012, URL: http://www.srf.ch/play/tv/arena/video/geld-fuer-alle-vision-oder-spinnerei?id=b657de9a-7fad-4920-953c-df1bfe5b59aa (05/30/2015).

[33] Michael Schoenenberger: Das Grundeinkommen raubt dem Menschen seine Freiheit, Neue Zürcher Zeitung, 04/13/2012, URL: http://www.nzz.ch/aktuell/startseite/das-grundeinkommen-raubt-dem-menschen-seine-freiheit-1.16412086 (05/30/2014).

[34] Rudolf Strahm: Süßer Traum: Das bedingungslose Grundeinkommen, Infosperber, 06/12/2012, URL: http://www.infosperber.ch/FreiheitRecht/Susser-Traum-Das-bedingungslose-Grundeinkommen (05/30/2015).

[35] Philipp Müller, Daniel Häni: "Epochale Entscheidung"—"Jeder Anreiz fällt weg," Aargauer Zeitung, 10/17/2012, URL: http://www.grundeinkommen.ch/wp-content/uploads/Aargauer_Zeitung_Mittwoch_17_Oktober_20121.pdf (05/30/2015).

[36] Katja Gentinetta: Freiheit für alle—Verantwortung für alle andern, philosophie.ch, 11/21/2014, URL: http://blogs.philosophie.ch/grundeinkommen/2014/11/21/freiheit-fuer-alle-verantwortung-fuer-alle-andern/ (05/30/2015).

[37] Reiner Eichenberger: "Ein Grundeinkommen führt zur Knechtschaft und nicht zur Freiheit," Neue Zürcher Zeitung, 12/06/2010, URL: http://www.nzz.ch/aktuell/startseite/ein-grundeinkommen-fuehrt-zur-knechtschaft-und-nicht-in-die-freiheit-1.8572095 (05/30/2015).

[38] Gregor Gysi: Frage zum Thema Demokratie und Bürgerrechte, abgeordnetenwatch.de, 11/26/2012, URL: http://www.abgeordnetenwatch.de/dr_gregor_gysi-575-37621--f362022.html#q362022 (05/30/2015).

[39] Beat Kappeler: Bedingungsloses Grundeinkommen ist unüberlegt, unliberal, asozial, Neue Zürcher Zeitung, 03/27/2011, URL: http://www.nzz.ch/aktuell/startseite/mein-standpunkt-bedingungsloses-grundeinkommen-ist-unueberlegt-unliberal-asozial-1.10040045 (05/30/2015).

[40] Christoph Mörgeli: Schlaraffenland und Steuerhölle, Weltwoche, no. 41/2013, URL: http://www.weltwoche.ch/ausgaben/2013-41/moergeli-schlaraffenland-und-steuerhoelle-die-weltwoche-ausgabe-412013.html (05/30/2015).

[41] Patrick Feuz: So werden wir nicht glücklicher, Tages-Anzeiger, 08/30/2014, URL: http://www.tagesanzeiger.ch/schweiz/standard/So-werden-wir-nicht-gluecklicher/story/22006694 (05/30/2015).

[42] Hansueli Schöchli: Per Dekret ins Paradies, Neue Zürcher Zeitung, 10/02/2013, URL: http://www.nzz.ch/aktuell/startseite/per-dekret-ins-paradies-1.18159926 (05/30/2015).

[43] Cf. Balz Ruchti, Yaël Debelle, Peter Johannes Meier: Geld für alle: Kann das gutgehen? Beobachter, no. 20/2013, URL: http://www.beobachter.ch/geld-sicherheit/sozialhilfe/artikel/bedingungsloses-grundeinkommen_geld-für-alle-kann-das-gutgehen/ (05/30/2015).

[44] Daniela Schneeberger: Das bedingungslose Grundeinkommen ist bedingungslos abzulehnen, Tages-Anzeiger, 10/14/2013, URL: http://politblog.tagesanzeiger.ch/blog/index.php/author/daniela-schneeberger/?lang=de (05/30/2015).

[45] Manfred Rösch: "Komfortable Stallfütterung," Finanz und Wirtschaft, 10/15/2013, URL: http://www.fuw.ch/article/komfortablestallfutterung-2/ (05/30/2015).

[46] Oswald Sigg, Corrado Pardini: Streit um eine Utopie, Tageswoche, 10/12/2012, URL: http://www.tageswoche.ch/de/2012_41/schweiz/469680/ (05/30/2015).

[47] Lukas Rühli: Einkommen ohne Grund. Warum das bedingungslose Grundeinkommen keines seiner Versprechen hält, avenir standpunkte, no. 5/2014, URL: http://www.avenir-suisse.ch/wp-content/uploads/2014/04/as_grundeinkommen_hp.pdf (05/30/2015).

[48] Rainer Hank, Götz W. Werner: Brüderlichkeit und Grundeinkommen: Wie funktioniert heute Solidarität?, SWR2 Forum, 09/02/2010, URL: http://www.swr.de/swr2/service/audio-on-demand/-/id=661264/did=6845716/pv=mplayer/vv=popup/nid=661264/dannw0/index.html (05/30/2015).

[49] Otfried Höffe: Das Unrecht des Bürgerlohns, Frankfurter Allgemeine Zeitung, 12/22/2007.

[50] Cf. Klipp & Klar: 150 Euro fürs Nichtstun! Grundeinkommen statt Hartz IV?, RBB, 09/26/2006, URL: http://www.rbb-online.de/_/klippundklar/beitrag_jsp/key=rbb_beitragex_4828440.html (05/30/2015).

[51] Wolfgang Kersting: Theorien der sozialen Gerechtigkeit, Stuttgart 2000, pp. 272f.

[52] Julian Nida-Rümelin: Zur Kritik der Idee eines bedingungslosen Grundeinkommens, Neue Gesellschaft/Frankfurter Hefte, no. 7-8/2008, URL: http://www.frankfurter-hefte.de/upload/Archiv/2008/Heft_07-08/NGFH_Jul-Aug_08_Archiv_Nida-Rmelin.pdf (05/30/2015).

[53] Angela Merkel: Enquete Kommission Grundeinkommen, direktzu.de, 02/08/2008, URL: http://www.direktzu.de/kanzlerin/messages/15587 (05/30/2015).

[54] Sahra Wagenknecht: Frage zum Thema Soziales, abgeordnetenwatch.de, 05/14/2008, URL: http://www.abgeordnetenwatch.de/sarah_wagenknecht_niemeyer-651-12385--f105280.html#q105280 (05/30/2015).

[55] Oswald Metzger: "Ich bin auf dem Sprung," Stern Online, 11/202007, URL: http://stern.de/politik/deutschland/oswald-metzger-ich-bin-auf-dem-sprung-603071.html (05/30/2015).

[56] Norbert Blüm: Wahnsinn mit Methode, Die Zeit, no. 17/2007, URL: http://www.zeit.de/2007/17/Grundeinkommen (05/30/2015).

[57] Heiner Flassbeck: Helikoptergeld—oder wer über das Kuckucksnest fliegt, flassbeck-economics, 03/11/2015, URL: http://www.flassbeck-economics.de/helikoptergeld-oder-wie-springt-man-ueber-das-kuckucksnest/?output=pdf (05/30/2015).

58 Cf. Schweizerischer Bundesrat: Botschaft zur Volksinitiative "Für ein bedingungsloses Grundeinkommen," Bundesblatt, no. 37/2014, URL: https://www.admin.ch/opc/de/federal-gazette/2014/6551.pdf (05/30/2015).

59 Bruno S. Frey: Wie vertragen sich direkte Demokratie und Wirtschaft?, Neue Zürcher Zeitung, 03/19/2014, URL: http://www.nzz.ch/meinung/debate/wie-vertragen-sichdirekte-demokratie-und-wirtschaft-1.18265687 (05/30/2015).

60 Andreas Gross: Das Grundeinkommen und das Selbstverständnis der Demokratie. Redebeitrag anlässlich der Basler Tagung der Stiftung Kulturimpuls Schweiz, 01/25/2014, URL: http://www.andigross.ch/ (05/30/2015).

61 Cf. Felix Schindler: Volk schmettert Mindestlohn ab, Tages-Anzeiger, 05/18/2014, URL: http://www.tagesanzeiger.ch/schweiz/standard/Volk-schmettert-Mindestlohn-ab/story/31933204 (05/30/2015).

62 Cf. Raphaela Birrer: 1:12-Initiative scheitert mit 65,3 Prozent, Tages-Anzeiger, 11/24/2013, URL: http://www.tagesanzeiger.ch/schweiz/standard/112Initiative-scheitert-mit-653-Prozent/story/12027169 (05/30/2015).

63 Stefan Brotbeck: Vergällte Freiheit? Zur Phänomenologie der Unfreiheit, in: Götz W. Werner, Peter Dellbrügger (eds.): Wozu Führung? Dimensionen einer Kunst, Karlsruhe 2014, p. 3; cf. Stefan Brotbeck: Heute wird nie gewesen sein. Aphorismen, Basel 2011, p. 129.

64 Cf. Peter Normann Waage: Ich. Eine Kulturgeschichte des Individuums, Stuttgart 2014.

65 Arno Widmann: Familie als Lebensabschnitt, Berliner Zeitung, 02/12/2014, URL: http://www.berliner-zeitung.de/meinung/leitartikel-zum-elternunterhalt-familie-als-lebensabschnitt,10808020,26175988.html (05/30/2015).

66 Gustav Radbruch: Vorschule der Rechtsphilosophie, Göttingen 1959, p. 25.

67 Thomas Paine: Agrarian Justice, in: Mark Philip (ed.): Thomas Paine: Rights of Man, Common Sense, and Other Political Writings, Oxford 1995, p. 420.

68 Cf. BIEN-Schweiz (ed.): Die Finanzierung eines bedingungslosen Grundeinkommens, Zurich 2010; Dirk Jacobi, Wolfgang Strengmann-Kuhn (eds.): Wege zum Grundeinkommen, Berlin 2012; Helmut Pelzer: Das bedingungslose Grundeinkommen. Finanzierung und Realisierung nach dem mathematisch fundierten Transfergrenzen-Modell, Stuttgart 2010; Thomas Straubhaar (ed.): Bedingungsloses Grundeinkommen und Solidarisches Bürgergeld—mehr als sozialutopische Konzepte, Hamburg 2008; André Presse: Grundeinkommen. Idee und Vorschläge zu seiner Realisierung, Karlsruhe 2010; Götz W. Werner, Wolfgang Eichhorn, Lothar Friedrich (eds.): Das Grundeinkommen. Würdigung—Wertungen—Wege, Karlsruhe 2012; Götz W. Werner, André Presse (eds.): Grundeinkommen und Konsumsteuer. Impulse für "unternimm die zukunft," Karlsruhe 2007.

69 Oswald von Nell-Breuning: Worauf es mir ankommt. Zur sozialen Verantwortung, Freiburg 1983, p. 62.

70 Cf. Daniel Häni, Enno Schmidt: Grundeinkommen. Das Heft zum Film, Basel 2008, p. 12.

[71] Cf. Max Weber: Wirtschaft und Gesellschaft. Grundriss der verstehenden Soziologie, Tübingen 2002.

[72] Cf. Hannah Arendt: Macht und Gewalt, Munich 2003.

[73] Götz W. Werner: "Das manische Schauen auf Arbeit macht uns alle krank," Stern, no. 17/2006, URL: http://stern.de/wirtschaft/job/grundversorgung-das-manische-schauen-auf-arbeit-macht-uns-alle-krank-560218.html (05/30/2015).

[74] Jean Ziegler: Zeit ist menschliches Leben, a tempo, no. 10/2006.

[75] Peter Ulrich: Der Kapitalismus hat nicht gesiegt, Südkurier, 05/21/2005, URL: http://www.aktive-demokraten.de/pdfs/Suedkurier-21-05-05.pdf (05/30/2015).

[76] Oswald Sigg: "Es braucht eine AHV ab dem ersten Lebensjahr!," Tages-Anzeiger, 08/27/2014, URL: http://www.tagesanzeiger.ch/schweiz/standard/Es-braucht-eine-AHV-ab-dem-ersten-Lebensjahr/story/29119687 (05/30/2015).

[77] Marina Weisband: "Vollbeschäftigung halte ich für rückständig," Kurier, 09/27/2013, URL: http://kurier.at/politik/ausland/marina-weisband-im-interview-ueber-politik-piraten-und-plaene/28.547.414 (05/30/2015).

[78] Cf. Eco: Klaus W. Wellershoff zum Grundeinkommen, Schweizer Fernsehen SRF, 04/18/2011, URL: http://www.srf.ch/play/tv/eco/video/klaus-wellershoff-zum-grundeinkommen?id=472cf99f-e8bc-4cfd-89a4-b6736f-6f0ab6 (05/30/2015).

[79] Linard Bardill: Debattiert, Leute! Coopzeitung, no. 20/2012, URL: http://www.coopzeitung.ch/3838704?rs.score=1&rs.name=pageRating&rs.item=cbi%3-A%2F%2F&2Fcms%2F3838707 (05/30/2015).

[80] Cf. Balz Ruchti, Yaël Debelle, Peter Johannes Meier: Geld für alle: Kann das gutgehen? Beobachter, no. 20/2013, URL: http://www.beobachter.ch/geld-sicherheit/sozialhilfe/artikel/bedingungsloses-grundeinkommen_geld-für-alle-kann-das-gutgehen/ (05/30/2015).

[81] Ralph Boes: Bedingungsloses Grundeinkommen—Wie ist das zu denken?, BbG Berlin, URL: http://www.buergerinitiative-grundeinkommen.de/fuer-grundeinkommen/sheets/TEXT%20WAHL.pdf (05/30/2015).

[82] Hans-Christian Ströbele: Frage zum Thema Soziales, abgeordnetenwatch.de, 11/24/2012, URL: http://www.abgeordnetenwatch.de/hans_christian_stroebele-575-37994--f361880.html#q361880 (05/30/2015).

[83] Katja Kipping: Trojanisches Pferd für 950 Euro, n-tv, 03/05/2009, URL: http://www.n-tv.de/politik/dossier/Trojanisches-Pferd-fuer-950-Euro-article5877-2.html (05/30/2015).

[84] Susanne Wiest: Rede vor dem Petitionsausschuss des Deutschen Bundestages, 11/08/2010, URL: http://www.archiv-grundeinkommen.de/petitionen/susanne-wiest/20101108-Rede-Susanne-Wiest-Bundestag-Petitionsausschuss.pdf (05/30/2015).

[85] Claus Offe: Familienleistung jenseits der Marktarbeit—das bedingungslose Grundeinkommen, in: Kurt Biedenkopf, Hans Bertram, Elisabeth Niejahr: Starke Familie—Solidarität, Subsidiarität und kleine Lebenskreise. Bericht der Kommis-

sion "Familie und demographischer Wandel" der Robert Bosch Stiftung, Stuttgart 2009, p. 134.

[86] Michael Opielka: Grundeinkommen als umfassende Sozialreform—Zur Systematik und Finanzierbarkeit am Beispiel des Vorschlags Solidarisches Bürgergeld, in: Thomas Straubhaar (ed.): Bedingungsloses Grundeinkommen und Solidarisches Bürgergeld—mehr als sozialutopische Konzepte, Hamburg 2008, p. 168.

[87] Theo Wehner, Sascha Liebermann: "Das bedingungslose Grundeinkommen macht nicht faul," Zeit Online, 12/30/2011, URL: http://www.zeit.de/politik/deutschland/2011-12/bedingungsloses-grundeinkommen-interview (05/30/2015).

[88] Dieter Althaus: Grundeinkommen für alle? Eine machbare Revolution, Die Welt, 11/26/2007, URL: http://www.welt.de/debatte/kommentare/article6070-690/Grundeinkommen-fuer-alle-Eine-machbare-Revolution.html (05/30/2015).

[89] Thomas Straubhaar: Warum Grundeinkommen gut zu den Piraten passt, Die Welt, 05/13/2013, URL: http://www.welt.de/wirtschaft/article116116985/Warum-Grundeinkommen-gut-zu-den-Piraten-passt.html (05/30/2015).

[90] Kurt Regotz: Zur Volksinitiative für ein bedingungsloses Grundeinkommen, Schiffbau Zurich, 04/21/2012, URL: https://vimeo.com/42200047 (05/30/2015).

[91] Richard David Precht: "Schafft die Parteien ab!," Cicero, no. 7/2009, URL: http://www.cicero.de/salon/%E2%80%9Eschafft-die-parteien-ab%E2%80%9C/39869 (05/30/2015).

[92] Sascha Liebermann: Freiheit ermöglichen, Solidarität stärken, Leistung fördern—durch ein bedingungsloses Grundeinkommen für alle Bürger, in: Daniela Schneckenburger (ed.): Freiheit statt Vollbeschäftigung? Ein Reader zur Debatte um bedingungsloses Grundeinkommen und Grundsicherung, Düsseldorf 2006, p. 27.

[93] Jakob Augstein: Fairness ist Zufall, Spiegel Online, 02/10/2011, URL: http://www.spiegel.de/politik/deutschland/s-p-o-n-im-zweifel-links-fairness-ist-zufall-a-7-44587.html (05/30/2015).

[94] Cf. Sternstunde Philosophie: David Graeber—Warum uns Schulden versklaven, Schweizer Fernsehen SRF, 10/13/2013, URL: http://www.srf.ch/play/tv/stern-stundephilosophie/video/david-graeber---warum-uns-schulden-versklaven?id=58a73fa9-24da-4068-ab1c-033cf285e590 (05/30/2015).

[95] Albert Wenger: Maschinen werden viele Jobs übernehmen, BR, 01/20/2015, URL: https://www.youtube.com/watch?v=xSBseloxS68&list=PLP4hePAK6Tv7S-qRSfofzB9u2IalA_iUS&index=1 (05/30/2015).

[96] Philipp Löpfe: Wir müssen jetzt ernsthaft über ein bedingungsloses Grundeinkommen sprechen, watson.ch, 01/11/2015, URL: http://www.watson.ch/!9000-46946 (05/30/2015).

[97] Enno Schmidt: Das ist mir zu philosophisch, philosophie.ch, 12/11/2014, URL: http://blogs.philosophie.ch/grundeinkommen/2014/12/11das-ist-mir-zu-philosophisch/ (05/30/2015).

[98] Adolf Muschg: Gespräch über das bedingungslose Grundeinkommen, Theater Neumarkt Zurich, 02/25/2012, URL: https://vimeo.com/37668072 (05/30/2015).

[99] Adolf Muschg: Der Mensch beginnt da, wo er etwas nicht muss, grundeinkommen.tv, 10/04/2012, URL: http://grundeinkommen.tv/adolf-muschg-zum-bedingungslosen-grundeinkommen/ (05/30/2015).

[100] Cf. Peter Sloterdijk: Streß und Freiheit, Berlin 2011, pp. 47f.

[101] Byung-Chul Han: Psychopolitik. Neoliberalismus und die neuen Machttechniken, Frankfurt 2014, p. 11.

[102] Cf. José Ortega y Gasset: Betrachtungen über die Technik. Der Intellektuelle und der Andere, Stuttgart 1949.

[103] Friedrich Schiller: Briefwechsel, Nationalausgabe, vol. 26, Weimar 1992, p. 299.

[104] Cf. Harry F. Harlow, Margaret Kuenne Harlow, Donald R. Meyer: Learning Motivated by a Manipulation Drive, Journal of Experimental Psychology, no. 40/1950, pp. 228-234, URL: http://psycnet.apa.org/journals/xge/40/2/228/ (05/30/2015).

[105] Cf. Edward L. Deci: Intrinsic Motivation, Extrinsic Reinforcement, and Inequity, Journal of Personality and Social Psychology, no. 22/1972, pp. 113-120, URL: http://www.selfdeterminationtheory.org/SDT/documents/1972_Deci_JPSP.pdf (05/30/2015).

[106] Cf. Edward L. Deci: Effects of Externally Mediated Rewards on Intrinsic Motivation, Journal of Personality and Social Psychology, no. 18/1971, pp. 105-115, URL: http://www.selfdeterminationtheory.org/SDT/documents/1971_Deci.pdf (05/30/2015).

[107] brand eins: Die Welt in Zahlen, no. 9/2009, URL: http://www.brandeins.de/archiv/2009/arbeit/ (05/30/2015).

[108] Lukas Rühli: "Ein unmoralisches Konzept," Pola rennt, 06/05/2014, URL: http://grundeinkommen.tv/pola-rennt-1-ein-unmoralisches-konzept-lukas-ruehli-avenir-suisse/ (05/30/2015).

[109] Michael Sennhauser: Grundeinkommen statt Lohn, Schweizer Radio DRS, 09/16/2008, URL: http://www.srf.ch/play/radio/popupaudioplayer?id=45cbfdf7-7938-4f7f-894c-e13724989bd9 (05/30/2015).

[110] Guido Kleinhubbert, Alexander Neubacher: Die Hartz-Fabrik, Der Spiegel, no. 1/2011, URL: http://magazin.spiegel.de/EpubDelivery/spiegel/pdf/76121041 (05/30/2015).

[111] Götz W. Werner: "Das manische Schauen auf Arbeit macht uns alle krank," Stern, no. 17/2006, URL: http://stern.de/wirtschaft/job/grundversorgung-das-manische-schauen-auf-arbeit-macht-uns-alle-krank-560218.html (05/30/2015).

[112] Heribert Prantl: Schikane per Gesetz, Süddeutsche Zeitung, 12/27/2014, URL: http://www.sueddeutsche.de/politik/jahre-hartz-iv-schikane-per-gesetz-1.2281699 (05/30/2015).

[113] Cf. Tagesschau: Wenn Arme keine Sozialhilfe beziehen, Schweizer Fernsehen SRF, 11/24/2012, URL: http://www.tagesschau.sf.tv/Nachrichten/Archiv/2012/ 11/24/Schweiz/Wenn-Arme-keine-Sozialhilfe-beziehen (05/30/2015).

[114] Lukas Rühli: Einkommen ohne Grund. Warum das bedingungslose Grundeinkommen keines seiner Versprechen hält, avenir standpunkte, no. 5/2014, URL: http://www.avenir-suisse.ch/wp-content/uploads/2014/04/as_grundeinkommen_hp.pdf (05/30/2015).

[115] Cf. Thomas Finkenauer (ed.): Sklaverei und Freilassung im römischen Recht, Berlin 2006; Elisabeth Herrmann-Otto: Sklaverei und Freilassung in der griechisch-römischen Welt, Hildesheim 2009.

[116] Cf. Manuel Alonso Olea: Von der Hörigkeit zum Arbeitsvertrag, Heidelberg 1981; Klaus Adomeit: Gesellschaftsrechtliche Elemente im Arbeitsverhältnis, Berlin 1986; Elisabeth Herrmann-Otto (ed.): Unfreie Arbeits- und Lebensverhältnisse von der Antike bis in die Gegenwart, Hildesheim 2005.

[117] Georg Kreisler: Meine Freiheit, deine Freiheit, URL: https://www.youtube.com/watch?v=u8-4n9yxZ_s (05/30/2015).

[118] Henrik Ibsen: Briefe, Berlin 1905, p. 159.

[119] Cf. Edelman Berland: Edelman Trust Barometer 2015, URL: http://www. edelman.com/news/trust-institutions-drops-level-great-recession/ (05/30/2015).

[120] Jürgen Habermas, Jacques Derrida: Philosophy in a Time of Terror, Chicago & London 2003, pp. 128f.

[121] Cf. Horst W. Opaschewski: Pädagogik der freien Lebenszeit, Opladen 1996.

[122] Friedrich Fröbel: Fortgesetzte Nachricht von der allgemeinen Deutschen Erziehungsanstalt in Keilhau, Rudolstadt 1823, p. 31.

[123] Cf. Duden: Freizeit, URL: http://www.duden.de/rechtschreibung/Freizeit (05/30/2015).

[124] Cf. Statista: Ernährte Personen durch einen Landwirt in Deutschland bis 2012, URL: http://de.statista.com/statistik/daten/studie/201243/umfrage/anzahl-der-menschen-die-durch-einen-landwirt-ernaehrt-werden/ (05/30/2015).

[125] Harald Welzer: Selbst denken. Eine Anleitung zum Widerstand, Frankfurt 2013, p. 219.

[126] Stefan Brotbeck: "Wir brauchen mehr Muße, um nicht zu verblöden," Basellandschaftliche Zeitung, 01/05/2013, URL: http://www.basellandschaftliche-zeitung.ch/basel/basel-stadt/philosoph-stefan-brotbeck-wir-brauchen-mehr-musse-um-nicht-zu-verbloeden-125868624 (05/30/2015).

[127] Ludwig Hohl: Die Notizen oder Von der unvoreiligen Versöhnung, Frankfurt 1984, p. 36.

[128] Ibid., p. 33.

www.ingramcontent.com/pod-product-compliance
Lightning Source LLC
Chambersburg PA
CBHW030446290526
45786CB00001B/461